To Ken + Marilynn!
Pots full of love —

EVERYDAY GOURMET

BlissPointBooks
Bliss Point Books
47 Maple St.,
Burlington, Vermont 05401
Bliss Point Books

ISBN Number: 978-0-9904592-2-4

Printed in the United States of America
First Edition: September 2014

Pots full of love to my wonderful family,

Jeff, Kate, Tuckie, Quinn & Fuad.

Thank you for cooking up these sweet

memories with me over the years.

And to my beloved mother, Pat Myette,

who sparked my love affair with the kitchen.

This book is a collection of some of my favorite family-oriented food columns that have appeared in The Williston Observer, Williston, Vermont over the past decade. When I began my 350-word bi-monthly column back in 2003, I invited new readers "…to release your inner gourmet; you'll find simple yet sophisticated ways to punch up your daily menus and entertainment plans… Together we'll make new food discoveries and techniques as easy and exciting as possible."

The original mantra for the *Everyday Gourmet* was (and remains) simple: "indulge your passion for food in some way, everyday. It takes just a small 'extra' to make an ordinary meal extraordinary. For example, chopping a handful of fresh herbs for a simple pasta dish will improve the meal threefold. Kosher salt, instead of table salt, is smarter. It is the 'traffic cop' of the food world and will organize and intensify flavors without making your food taste salty. When a dish is too spicy, sour, or salty, add a dab or two of maple syrup to rebalance the flavors." And so on… for over three hundred columns.

As a writer, it was a real challenge for me to show up at the page and create the columns on a deadline. Often I would angst over them so much that it made my stomach ache, but when I just relaxed and wrote about what I was actually cooking in my kitchen that day, the words flowed easily. So much has changed on the food landscape in recent years. Where once grains, pasta, and the food pyramid ruled, we now have gluten-free primal eating, the locavore movement, and craft beers. It has been a real education to follow the trends, science, and evolution of eating; I am indebted to *The Everyday Gourmet* column for keeping me at the table, always hungry for more.

Chatting with foodie friends and risk-adversive busy moms over the years, I learned that many cooks were reluctant to try new things due to time constraints, or they feared the kids (or hubby) might hate it. My goal was to introduce new food trends and bullet-proof techniques, making mealtime as easy and healthy as possible. The stories in this collection are from the heart, chronicling activity and mealtime in our busy household as my husband, Jeff, and I raised three precociously food-savvy daughters: Kate, Tuckie and Quinn. The recipes and techniques in this book are simple yet exciting, and they are rooted in classical French technique.

I was blessed to be raised by parents who were passionate about food and wine. My mother, Pat Myette, is an exquisite self-taught cook, so I was always learning about the good stuff from a very young age. She was the first person in our neighborhood to subscribe to Gourmet magazine back in the '60's, a true cooking rebel. Growing up, I remember that my family had the (annoying to some) habit of talking about the next amazing feast we were going to create spank in the middle of an already terriffic meal. Passion and enthusiasm were bountiful at our table. As an emerging adult I learned much about the execution and presentation of food and wine while working in professional and home kitchens. Always curious about the technical aspect of cooking, I was lucky enough to study at La Varenne Cooking School with Anne

Willan in Burgundy, France, and I completed the La Varenne Professionals Course in 1995.

I believe food is a wonderful gift that people give to each other in a connected community, and the quality of that act permeates every level of our busy everyday lives when there is often not enough time or energy to go around. This collection is a sentimental survey of my passion for the power of food to gather, heal, celebrate, and inspire those I love.

Kim Dannies

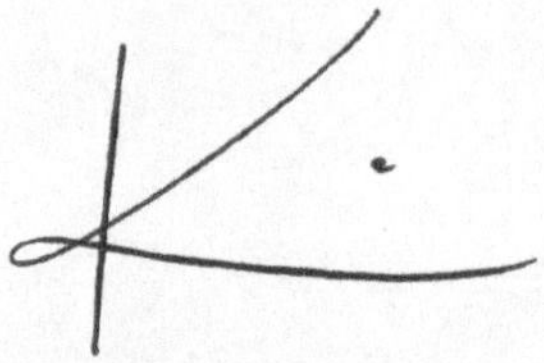

Williston, Vermont 2014

2003

EVERYDAY GRANOLA

MARCH 13, 2003

I love to exercise almost as much as I love to eat, and my Everyday Granola Recipe is the embodiment of both passions. It wasn't until I started riding a bicycle seriously that I began to appreciate the body's need for a good breakfast. This perfect fuel stays with me all morning long: it is crunchy, healthful, and delicious! I start each day with a bowlful topped with antioxidant-rich blueberries and vanilla soy milk. A nice benefit of this satisfying cereal is that I don't crave cookies and sweets as much, which keeps me on track with my fitness goals.

Toasting releases the natural oils and aromas of the ingredients and adds fantastic flavor and complexity to the cereal. This makes a wonderful hostess or holiday gift for friends and family. Play with the proportions to your liking.

EVERYDAY GRANOLA

Preheat oven to 350°F. Line 2 cookie sheets with parchment paper, spread 1 42–ounce container of Quaker Old Fashioned Oats evenly between the pans; toast for 25 minutes. Add the oats to a very large prep bowl.

Toast 2 14–ounce packages of flaked coconut until light brown in color, about 12 minutes. Watch it carefully, stirring half way through toasting. Add to oats.

Lightly crush 3–cups of whole almonds, and 3–cups of pecans, toast for about 20 minutes, stirring half way through. Repeat with sunflower and sesame seeds. Add to oat mixture along with some dried fruits such as raisins, cherries, blueberries and cranberries (optional).

The granola will smell delicious. Cool the batch, then fill 1–quart freezer bags with the granola and store in the freezer until ready for use.

When you really must have a cookie—and we all do from time to time—add this granola as your secret ingredient to my Green Mountain Chocolate Chip Cookies. Simply make a double batch of the tollhouse package recipe and add 3–4 handfuls of this granola to the batter.

A CLASSIC RITE OF SPRING

APRIL 10, 2003

Baby rack of lamb is a wonderful early spring meal—the meat is serious food, yet the colorful lemon, herb, and asparagus create a refreshing spark for both eye and palate. Purchase rack of lamb from a butcher and ask for it "frenched" (or buy a rack for two at Costco) which makes slicing the chops easier. Serve with Sherry Mushroom Sauce and roasted root vegetables smothered in fresh thyme, olives, and kosher salt. One rack serves two hearty appetites; portion meat and vegetable quantities to your needs.

BABY RACK OF LAMB

Pre-heat oven to 425°F. Lightly glaze a roasting pan with olive oil, and place two lemon-sized chunks of cauliflower, some cubed red potatoes, and the rack of lamb in the pan. Place sprigs of rosemary, sliced garlic, and lemon slices over the food. Sprinkle with kosher salt. Roast the food for 15 minutes.

Meanwhile, in a small food processor, combine 4–garlic cloves; 2–slices of baguette; and a handful of de-stemmed parsley, process well.

After 15 minutes, remove the roasting pan from oven, and place on a heatproof surface. Be careful: it's very hot! Smear 2–T of Dijon mustard over the lamb and pack the breadcrumb mixture over the mustard paste. Turn the vegetables and coat with juices. Return to oven and roast for 20 minutes longer.

SHERRY SAUCE

Melt 1–T of butter in sizzling non-stick sauté pan and cook 2–cups of sliced mushrooms for 3 minutes. Add 1–cup of quality sherry (not cooking sherry, it's too salty) to the pan and deglaze, scraping up bits of mushrooms, let simmer until reduced by half. Add 1–T of cream and stir with a whisk until bubbling but not boiling.

Steam asparagus for 10 minutes. Sprinkle with kosher salt and fresh pepper, and lemon wedges.

Remove lamb from oven and let it rest for 5 minutes. Toss vegetables with thyme, olives, and salt. Slice lamb into chops and plate to serve with vegetables. Serve sherry sauce on the side. Serves 2–3.

NANTUCKET NOSH

APRIL 23, 2003

This week's Spring Break finds my family enjoying the quiet and beauty of tiny Nantucket Island, whose population will more than quadruple during the summer months. Savoring freshly caught seafood, empty beaches and long rides on the bike path, our main preoccupation is "what's for dinner?" I've endured some ribbing about it, but the most important item I packed for this trip is my cast-iron frying pan. I always cook fish and seafood outside on a hot grill. The cast iron fires up nicely to seal in cooking juices and flavor, and no fishy fumes haunt the kitchen later. Here is today's menu.

CREAMY LEMON PASTA

Boil water. In a large bowl place the zest and juice of 2–lemons, salt and pepper to taste. Stir in 1–cup of crème fraiche or heavy cream. Cook 1–pound of fettuccini for 11 minutes. Drain and add pasta to lemon mixture, toss well.

CAPESANTE AL PESTO

Dry 1–pound of sea scallops on paper towel. In a shallow bowl measure ½–cup flour and season with 2–T Old Bay Seasoning.

Pesto: In a food processor place 2–cups fresh basil leaves; 3–garlic cloves; ½–cup toasted pine nuts; and ½–cup freshly shredded parmesan cheese. Pulse together until combined well. With motor running, drizzle in ½–cup extra virgin olive oil until a paste-like consistency is achieved, 1 minute or so. Adjust for flavor with salt and pepper. Pour into a small serving bowl.

Heat up the grill and place cast-iron pan on it, close the hood. Wait 2 minutes and then add ⅓–cup olive oil. Toss scallops in seasoned flour, and when the oil is popping hot, add them to pan; beware of oil splattering; close hood. Sear for 1 minute. Open up grill hood, put on heat protection for your hand, then give the pan a couple of vigorous shakes. The scallops should be browning nicely for a total cooking time of 2–3 minutes.

Plate pasta and then portion scallops and top with pesto. Serves 4.

MOTHER MAY I?

MAY 8, 2003

Here's some advice for family members who are thinking about cooking up something special for Mother's Day: the first thing you should know about Mother's Day is that even though it is supposed to be a holiday for Mom, it has the potential of becoming a very stressful day for her. Mothers are used to orchestrating holidays, planning meals, and generally running the show, so to take her out of the action is not necessarily a guaranteed treat. It's kind of like President Bush telling General Tommy Franks "go ahead and take that vacation now that the Iraqi invasion is underway."

How do we please the conflicted party girl without suffering casualties from friendly fire? The key is to convey competence. Start by planning a homemade gourmet meal, but remember that this kind of food is good only when it is superior in taste to its store-bought counterparts. Wisdom dictates adopting some no-fail shortcut strategies to ensure a dinner victory. Start with a crisp chardonnay: set Mom up in her favorite chair and pop the cork.

Now, prep the hors d'oeuvres. Pre-purchase a variety of olives from the deli, grab a container of hummus and a bag of baby carrots, toast some pita bread and snap into chips. Plate the goodies, and Viola! The party has begun.

Now, dump some boneless chicken breasts into a Ziploc bag, pour Ken's Lite Caesar dressing over them, and marinate for a few minutes, while you quarter-cut colored peppers and a couple of red onions. Place the veggies in a second Ziploc bag and add some more of the dressing.

Fire up the grill. Cook some boxed Rice Pilaf and add a small can of spiced and diced tomatoes for firepower. (15 minutes to go 'til you're a hero.) Grill the veggies and chicken, and arrange on a serving platter with the rice.

You are now in the home stretch: bring out the beautiful cake you remembered to buy yesterday, toast your smiling Queen, and smother her with kisses.

TAPAS IN SPAIN

JUNE 19, 2003

¡Hola from glorious Sevilla! The city that gave birth to opera legends Carmen, Don Juan, and Figaro runs full throttle on pure passion all day, everyday. I am visiting this exquisite wonderland to travel with our seventeen-year-old, an exchange student in the Andalusia region. Kate is my food muse, and I've missed her appetite and enthusiasm greatly these past five months. We are making up for lost time by eating our way through Spain, our palates providing a magic carpet for discovery and pleasure.

The Sevilla tapas bars are the most fun and reasonable way to eat as we absorb big doses of the spicy Castilian culture. The tapas tradition began when a small plate was placed upon bar drinks to keep the flies out. Happily this practice evolved into three delectable bites appearing on the plate, the offering just about any kind of yummy: batter fried squid, prawns with white beans in veal sauce, sherry and garlic steamed clams, Bellota ham, aged Manchego cheese, spicy grilled chorizo (sausage), olives, chickpeas with spinach, or even cola de toro (stewed oxtail).

When the barman barks "Digame" ("tell me!") be ready with a rapid response or starve. I defer to fluent Kate to handle the tapas order. Among the vast array she spots her favorite traditional dish, Tortilla Español, a simple, earthy potato pie that is eaten with the same frequency and gusto that we typically consume pizza or frites. More like a potato omelet, it is classic tapas eaten with ketchup and mayo. ¡Buen Provecho!

TORTILLA ESPAÑOL

Heat oven to 425ºF. Mince 3–4 garlic cloves. Dice a medium sized onion and sauté in olive oil for 5 minutes until lightly browned. Thinly slice 4–6 potatoes and place half in an oiled cast iron pan or round baking dish. Sprinkle with kosher salt and pepper and half of the cooked onion and minced garlic. Repeat process pressing down lightly on the potatoes. Place in hot oven and cook for 18 minutes. Sprinkle ½–cup of a favorite cheese over the dish and bake for 15–18 minutes more. Slice like a pie and serve on small plates, tapas style.

A COOK'S SECRET WEAPONS

JULY 30, 2003

A good cook knows that to elevate a dish from ordinary to extraordinary it takes a little "extra". I call my "extras" the seven wonders of the kitchen world and a combination of these ingredients makes the food I cook extraordinary in some way, everyday. My seven kitchen wonders happen to be garlic, olive oil, citrus, herbs, sea salt, crème fraiche, and balsamic syrup.

Take a moment to think about what combination of core ingredients inspires your artistry in the kitchen, and stock up. You may be wondering about the balsamic syrup: it is a simple reduction of cheap balsamic vinegar that delivers all the wonderful tang of vinegar without the awful bang. A simple process transforms it into a beautiful mahogany colored elixir that adds zip and sophistication to just about any dish. Wine lovers adore it because they can enjoy a vinaigrette dressed salad that won't spoil wine's flavor on their palate.

Health conscious cooks use it as a secret weapon for adding flavor instead of fat (my Mom adds 2–T to her famous chicken soup stock). Cooks love it for the vast array of foods that are instantly enhanced by the nutty, slightly sweet and tangy essence of the syrup. Drizzle it on everything from grilled veggies to strawberries and ice cream, you'll feel like Picasso with new paint: extraordinary!

BALSAMIC SYRUP

In a large non-stick sauté pan combine 1–32 ounce (or larger) bottle of cheap balsamic vinegar (I use the Costco bottle);

2 –T brown sugar; a pinch of cinnamon (or customize with your favorite spice).

Simmer on medium. The fumes may be strong, initially, so turn on your exhaust fan. Simmer for 20–25 minutes, stirring occasionally, and monitoring it more carefully as time elapses. The vinegar will have increasing bubble formations on the surface as the reduction is completed.

When the vinegar thickly coats the back of a metal spoon and remains there, you are at the syrup stage. Turn off heat and let the balsamic syrup cool and thicken. (If it is too thick, simply add a bit of water.) Pour into an attractive vessel that is readily available in your cooking area. Use it on everything!

007 CHEESE CAKE

JULY 18, 2003

Did you know that we have our own international food celebrity right here in Williston? That's right, it's Bob Reese of the Vermont Butter & Cheese Company. Not many would guess that this funny, mild mannered, devoted father of three boys actually leads a double life as the James Bond of the dairy world.

You may find Bob hobnobbing with New York City's top chefs one week, consulting in Bosnia the next or, wait, is he at Chicago's Fancy Food show this week? (We are never quite sure where to find our dashing Bob.)

He and his business partner, Allison Hooper, own one of the world's most successful specialty food companies. From tiny Websterville, Vermont they produce award winning goat cheeses, crème fraiche, fromage blanc, mascarpone and butter. Their Impastata Creamy Goat Cheese won first place at the 2002 World Cheese Championships and the luscious butter (86% butter fat), won the 2002 American Cheese Society's blue ribbon.

While we can only dream of the food flirtations Bob has experienced over the past two decades in the business, we can grab a little slice of the action right here in Williston by visiting Adams Farm Market and treating ourselves to Vermont Butter & Cheese products.

TZATZIKI (TA-ZEE-KI)

This Greek dip is healthful, fast, and fabulous when made with Vermont Butter & Cheese fromage blanc, a fat-free cow's milk cheese. Mix ingredients together and pair Tzatziki with baked pita chips.

Combine 2 8–ounce containers of fromage blanc (strain excess water from container); 1–cucumber seeded and grated (wrap in paper towel to squeeze out water); 4–minced garlic cloves; zest of one lemon; 2–t olive oil; 2–t lemon juice; Sea salt, to taste. To serve, top with extra shredded cucumber and lemon slices. Yield: 2 cups.

FRESH START FOR FALL

AUGUST 28, 2003

I caught a bad case of the back to school buzz while I was at Staples this morning and now I'm in a fever pitch to clean my kitchen. Just like my kids with their fresh notebooks and sharp pencils, I want to feel renewed and ready for fall.

I'm making an audit by scrubbing down every surface and re-evaluating equipment needs. I'm cleaning out drawers and cabinets and tossing the stuff I haven't used in six months. While I work, I make a grocery list to restock the pantry, and I'll pick up some fun items to experiment with such as curry paste and sesame tahini.

Any excess pans or utensils go to the refugee resettlement project. If I recycle my massive cookbook collection, I'll have room for the new volumes that are forming tall cairns around my home. My favorite arrival is *A New Way to Cook* by Sally Schneider; it's the *Joy of Cooking* for the 21st century. I won't forget to repot herbs, add some pretty mums to brighten things up, and refill grain jars with new product from Healthy Living: bulgur, barley, couscous, a variety of rice, beans and lentils (the tiny French green ones, not the brown!).

As a reward, I'll take a field trip to Fresh Market on Pine Street to restock our wine rack with delicious bargains. Afterward I'll cross the parking lot to Great Harvest Breads and grab a couple of their delectable loaves made with freshly milled flours, perfect to serve with my savory French Lentil Salad. You know, I'm beginning to like this back to school buzz, keep it coming!

FRENCH LENTIL SALAD

Boil 5–cups of water and add 2–cups of green French Lentils, cook covered for 17 minutes. Strain and pour into a prep bowl.

In a food processor chop 3–4 garlic cloves; add 4–T of Dijon mustard; ½–cup red wine vinegar; kosher salt and fresh pepper to taste. Pulse lightly. With motor running, drizzle in ¾–cup of excellent olive oil. Adjust seasoning for taste; it should exude a pungent flavor. Pour dressing over cooled lentils; mix well, then plate portions.

For added protein: in a little oil, sear 8–ounces of shrimp or scallops on high heat; portion over the lentils. Serve with freshly sliced tomatoes, lemons, and a pinch of sea salt. Serves 3 large or 6 small plates.

KATE'S FIRST KISS CAKE

SEPTEMBER 11, 2003

Today we remember and comfort one another, the horrors of 9/11 still fresh in our collective memory. What better way to cobble together week-weary friends and family than with a deep dark chocolaty cake? This chocolate cake is the best I've ever baked. It's easy to make: you'll notice that it begins with a commercial mix. (Anytime I can save time with a product that is equal to or better than my own effort, I am all for it.)

Just a word of caution about this recipe: upon consumption it will cause people to move about your home in a spellbound fog, searching for that second piece of cake. They will do the dishes without being asked, they will promote world peace, and yes, they may even fall in love with you, returning for a kiss (and another piece of cake.) What could be more comforting than that?

KATE'S FIRST KISS CHOCOLATE CAKE

Preheat oven to 350° F. Spray 3–9" cake pans with non-stick spray.

Beat together one devils' food cake mix with 1 ⅓ cups water; 3 eggs; ½–cup vegetable oil; 3–T Kirsch liqueur; and 1–t almond extract in a large bowl.

Mix in 1–cup chocolate chips. Divide batter among the three pans, bake about 15–18 minutes until tester comes out clean. Cool cake for 10 minutes and then invert onto cooling racks.

Combine ½–cup butter and ¼–cup cream in a small saucepan. Stir over medium low heat until butter melts and mixture comes to a light simmer. (Do not let it boil!)

Place 2 cups of chocolate chips in a glass bowl, microwave on high for 1 ½ minutes, stir. Remove cream from the heat and gently whisk in chocolate and 3–T of Kirsch. Cool until just barely warm and beat in 1–2 cups of confectionery sugar starting with 1 cup, and adding more as you gauge the consistency.

When cakes and frosting are completely cool, frost first layer, stack a second one, frost, and repeat for third layer. Top with 1 cup slivered almonds or toasted coconut if you like. Allow cake to set for a few hours. Serve with very cold milk (and some supervision!)

A MAN FOR ALL MENUS

OCTOBER 9, 2003

It's wine harvest time and a nice opportunity to celebrate a change of season. My eighty-six year-old father-in-law is visiting this weekend to celebrate his birthday. Bob 'Popop' Dannies loves to eat and drink well. I call him the Silver Fox because he is as fit and handsome as he was when I married his son twenty years ago. What is his secret to a long healthy life?

He enjoys himself at table with no inhibitions and balances that pleasure with lots of outdoor exercise and lively conversation peppered with curiosity. A couple of times a week Popop treats himself to a short martini before lunch; he swears that it is the best antidote to the bacon and sausage he adores. All of his favorites are on the birthday menu: beef tenderloin with roasted red onions, maple butternut squash, and garlic roasted red potatoes.

I'm also making a new recipe to surprise him. If you've never been crazy about cauliflower before, this dish will convert you. It is a wonderful way to combine the last of the tomatoes with fresh cauliflower in a golden, crunchy breadcrumb shell.

For wine, a 2001 Vieilles Vignes Sancerre will open the palate, followed by a gold medal 1996 Rosemount Cabernet Sauvignon Coonawarra. Apple Crostada and ice cream should finish us off…everyone, except of course, Popop!

CAULIFLOWER & TOMATO GRATIN

Start with a head of fresh cauliflower and slice off the bottom stem, but keep it intact. Rinse cauliflower, place upright in a glass pie plate, cover with plastic, and microwave for 10–12 minutes on high.

Remove plastic and place a pint of cherry tomatoes around the edges of cauliflower. Melt ½–cup butter and pour one third of it over the cauliflower. Season the cauliflower with kosher salt and freshly ground pepper, to taste.

Toast 2–3 slices of whole grain bread, crusts cut off, and process in a Cuisinart along with 2–small garlic cloves and 1–cup of Parmesan cheese. Pat the breadcrumb and cheese mixture over the entire surface and drizzle remainder of the butter all over. Bake uncovered in a 350°F oven for 30–40 minutes until bubbling and golden. Serves 6–8.

COLD WEATHER COMFORT FOOD

NOVEMBER 6, 2003

Beef stroganoff is the food equivalent of my favorite winter sweater, a hearty comfort meal that's always first choice for brisk November evenings. I like it for busy nights when my gang eats in shifts, or when I want to treat my friends to something that is at once casual and special.

It is a perennial family favorite; even a picky eater like my daughter, Tuckie, would eat this stew everyday, if offered. The rich flavor comes from the caramelized onions, mushrooms, and sherry. For ultimate flavor, cook the onions on medium heat until they are nicely browned and shiny, this is the signal that they have released their natural sugars. Caramelization takes 15–20 minutes, and a little stirring.

The next step is to deglaze the pan by pouring good quality drinking sherry into the pan over heat. Using a wooden spatula, scrape up all the browned bits; these gems are loaded with color and flavor. By repeating this process with the mushrooms and the meat, you'll be utilizing a simple technique that is a chef's secret for building complex flavor into a basic sauce; the extra effort will take your cooking to the next level of flavor and sophistication. (A nice vegetarian alternative is to substitute chunky cut portabella mushrooms for the meat.)

TUCKIE'S BEEF STROGANOFF

Heat a large non-stick sauté pan with 1–T olive oil. Dice a large yellow onion and cook onion until caramelized 15–20 minutes. Deglaze with ⅓–cup of good sherry. Scrape every molecule into a glass bowl, reserve.

Repeat process with 1–pound sliced mushrooms. Add to reserved onions. Cut 1–pound sirloin steak into bite sized chunks. Heat the pan to medium-hi and sear the meat for 2 minutes, moving chunks vigorously in the pan and scraping up browned bits. Deglaze with ⅓–cup sherry, let it simmer on medium heat.

Add 1–can cream of mushroom soup; ⅓–cup Dijon mustard; and 3–T of crème fraiche or full fat sour cream. Stir well. Add 4–minced garlic cloves and the reserved onions and mushrooms. Stir and simmer for 2 minutes, season with salt and pepper to taste.

Pour mixture into a covered casserole dish. This dish is a great do-ahead as it keeps well for up to three days at this point. To serve, heat in oven at 350°F for 45 minutes. Serve over 1–pound of extra-wide egg noodles cooked al dente; top with freshly chopped parsley. Serves 6–8.

2004

COZY THAI TIME

JANUARY 22, 2004

During this freezing weather I usually eat higher calorie comfort foods for fuel, but the pate and truffle blitz I staged during the holidays is making it tough to fit into my favorite jeans. My new strategy for staying warm, while warding off the saddlebag syndrome, is the hot 'n spicy Asian antidote.

Tonight I'll be snuggling in with a chili spiked chicken Pad Thai while I watch The Apprentice. (I hope Donald Trump's hairdo won't give me indigestion again this week). The complex flavors, ease of preparation, and refreshing ingredients in Pad Thai always cheer me up and leave me feeling pleasantly satisfied, not stuffed. I use generous amounts of fresh ginger root, a wonderful wintertime spice: ginger generates internal warmth, clears the palate and settles the digestive system.

Buy a knob of ginger root in the produce section and peel it like an apple, inhaling its' wonderful perfume. Cut it up into chunks, and then mince the ginger in a small food processor. Pour the ginger into a glass jar and cover it with good quality sherry; store it in the fridge. You'll have freshly minced ginger root ready to use at a moment's notice. The chili garlic sauce and Pad Thai rice noodles are in the specialty section of the supermarket; I prefer the fettuccini cut for a heartier wintertime dish.

CHILI SPIKED CHICKEN PAD THAI

In a large sauté pan, heat 1–T of coconut oil and sauté one large diced onion and 8–ounces of sliced mushrooms together for 15 minutes, until caramelized.

Prep condiments into small individual serving bowls: scramble 2–eggs; toast 1–cup coconut; 1–cup chopped peanuts; ½–cup chili garlic sauce; 2–c fresh bean sprouts; ½–cup sliced scallions. Reserve on a tray.

To the onion batch add ½–cup each chopped carrot and celery; 4–minced garlic cloves; 2–T fresh ginger; 1–14 ounce can of coconut milk; 2–T garlic chili sauce; and 1–cup chicken stock, simmer for 5 minutes.

Meanwhile, boil water and cook 1–pound of Pad Thai rice noodles al dente; drain and reserve. To the Pad Thai batch add 1–pound of cubed chicken breasts; simmer 3 minutes. Fold in cooked noodles and simmer 3 minutes more. Place steaming contents into a large serving bowl. Serve with condiments. Serves 6.

A BOWL FULL OF SOUL

FEBRUARY 5, 2004

Making soup is a lot like playing jazz. You begin with a few standards and pretty soon you can't keep track of the improvisations. Jazz is America's only original living art form, it is expressive and it is enriching, and so it was with tonight's soup.

It began with the standard French mirepoix of onion, celery, carrot, and garlic, and before long, we were eating a bowl full of soul: Santa Fe White Bean Soup. I found some fennel, a sexy cousin to celery, in the crisper along with a bit of corn and some fresh salsa that was sitting next to the leftover grilled chicken, and so we started to jam–all the way to Santa Fe. (I only picked that name because it is a sunny and divine place to be–my cabin fever blues at a fever pitch just now).

The stock was easy: I sautéed the mirepoix and fennel in a little butter for 15 minutes, then deglazed with a splash or two of sherry. I added a can of diced Tuttorosso brand tomatoes, along with the chicken stock, a couple of cans of rinsed cannellini beans, corn, salsa, and chicken.

Pro tip: place one-third of the soup into a large food processor, let it cool a bit, then pulse the mixture gently until almost processed, you know the beat. Return it to the pot and adjust for seasoning with kosher salt and pepper.

Now, here is where we really got to the swing: just before serving, I placed a large handful of chopped fresh spinach, parsley, and fennel foliage into the pot and let it wilt slightly. It's a beautiful thing to see: that steaming soup in the bowl, the gorgeous colors, textures, and flavors, and then cool mound of shredded Asiago cheese on top, all coming together to make beautiful music for the mouth. Dig in, man, it's hot!

SANTA FE WHITE BEAN SOUP SHOPPING LIST:

2–large onions, chopped; 4–ribs of celery, chopped; 4–carrots, diced; 4–cloves garlic, minced; 4–ribs fresh fennel, chopped; 1–can corn, drained; 8–ounces fresh medium salsa; 2–cups cooked chicken, cubed (optional); 1–16 ounce can of diced tomatoes; 4–cups of chicken stock; 2–cans of cannellini beans, drained; 2–cups fresh spinach; parsley and fennel foliage, chopped; 1–cup shredded Asiago or parmesan cheese. Serves 8.

THE SECRET LIVES OF DENTISTS

MARCH 4, 2004

For every passionate cook there comes a point when the desire for knowledge about the deeper nuances of cooking burns so intently that it becomes an obsession. The symptoms include a constant preoccupation with chemistry, daydreaming about career changes, and the hoarding of cookbooks.

I was talking with my dentist, Williston resident Dr. Paul Averill, recently, and I could tell by the wild look in his eye as he peppered me with cooking questions that he was in the advanced stages of the cooking obsession. Concerned for his welfare, I invited him and a few cooking buddies over for an intervention, um, I mean a cooking lesson. Learning the following "secrets" seemed to bring him a measure of relief.

One good sharp knife is better than a block full of dull knives.

Kosher salt applied sparingly in stages is far better for creating and controlling flavors than simply using table salt at the end of the cooking process.

Freshly chopped garlic is crucial to flavor quality; please Paul: *No jar garlic!*

Fresh herbs like parsley, mint, and thyme are recipe enhancers; use liberally.

Fresh herbs such as dill, rosemary, cilantro, and sage are concentrated recipe enhancers; use more conservatively.

Good quality olive oil can be used for everything, including baking.

Heat a non-stick sauté pan before adding oil; add 1–t of oil and heat it before adding food. You'll use less oil, and the food will cook better. Use butter to finish sauces at the end of the cooking process—you'll enjoy more of the butter's flavor.

Penzey's Spices sells a diverse array of blended spice combinations for pennies; stock up on a few different small jars each month.

Ken's Steak House Lite Caesar dressing is an excellent marinade for grilled chicken or fish. Be sure to wrap grilled food in a double layer of heavy duty foil, and let the food "rest" for at least 20 minutes before serving, for maximum juiciness.

Proper caramelization of onions and mushrooms can occur only after 15–20 minutes of heat. Use wine or stock to deglaze the pan and to create a sauce.

Although I had a great time during our cooking lesson, I must admit that I did have an ulterior motive when I offered to teach Dr. Paul. For all concerned, I wanted to derail any notions of a potential career change—he is, after all, a damn good dentist.

RENEWING FRIENDSHIPS WITH FINE FOOD

APRIL 15, 2004

I invited friends for lunch to get reacquainted after winter's marathon of schizoid schedules, compulsive carpooling, and impotent weather. Our lives are over-full as the demands of parenting and work keep us at full throttle; ipso facto, we are all habitual offenders of recycling recipes that bore us to tears.

For this rare summit I planned the menu around my five-fingered formula for sharing food: it must be healthy, delicious, fresh, beautiful, and interesting. I visited Healthy Living to get the cornerstone ingredient, whole wheat bulgur. I gave our beloved Tabouli, typically a tomato season specialty, a spring make-over and the results were exciting. It is superb with roasted tomatoes at this time of year.

Just like the food, the joy and delight we took in each other's company that day was immensely satisfying. Whoever says that "food is love" really knows what they are talking about.

SPRINGTIME TABOULI

Toss 4–cups of grape or cherry tomatoes tomatoes in 2–T olive oil place on a cookie sheet, lightly sprinkle kosher salt and granulated garlic over the batch. Roast tomatoes in a 400°F oven for 1 hour, shaking the cookie sheet every 20 minutes.

Place 4–cups of whole wheat bulgur in a large bowl and pour boiling water over until the water just covers it. Let it set for 10 minutes; fluff with a chopstick. Toss in remaining ingredients: 2–cups each chopped scallions, fresh mint, and parsley; the zest of 5–lemons with their juices; salt and pepper to taste. Fold in roasted tomatoes. Serve in a wide, flat bowl with grilled chicken breasts on side. Serves 8–12.

LOVE AT FIRST BITE

MAY 13, 2004

There's a new guy in town, and I want to date him every night. Never mind that I've been married for twenty years, this really wouldn't qualify as cheating. More like eating. His name is Nicco's Cucina and he is serving up some of the best food I've eaten, anywhere. Nicco's lives at the new Maple Tree Place. He is hip, relaxed, and easy on the eye with handsome Italian coloring, a warm airy space, and a hospitable bar area to wait if things are running a bit late—Nicco's doesn't do reservations. I like everything about him, from the delectable antipasto di mare bursting with shrimp, tuna, and fresh mozzarella, to the racy Abruzzi Napoli-style thin crust stone hearth pizza.

The pizza, this is where I really fell in love. I haven't tasted pizza like this since Naples, 1980; this is pizza you daydream about. The crust is thin and crispy and pops in your mouth. Toppings like roasted sweet sausage, prosciutto di Parma, sweet red onion, and baby clams are all tempting. Nicco's knows that less is more, and suggests three toppings, max, for ultimate flavor. Soup, salads, pasta and the Della Cucina menu are all expertly prepared by Chef Frank Pace, a Napa–trained, Italian-Vermonter.

Since I can't get a kitchen pass to visit Nicco's every day, I'll have to bridge the gap with some homemade pizza. My dear friend and longtime business partner, Judy Marschke, makes the best home-version I've ever tasted. She says that the key to good pizza dough is to knead it by hand with lots of TLC. This step gives the dough a crunchy and light texture that will make your homemade pizza love-at-first-bite.

JUDY MARSCHKE'S HOMEMADE PIZZA DOUGH

1–packet of dry yeast combined with ⅔ cup warm water

2–T olive oil

2–cups white flour (excellent with ½ white and ½ whole wheat also)

Combine ingredients in a large bowl and mix well, by hand.

When dough is formed, place in a resting bowl that has been lightly greased with additional olive oil. Dough will be soft and slightly sticky. Let dough rise until triple in bulk. Punch down and stretch over pizza pans that have been lightly greased with olive oil. Use fresh tomatoes, mushrooms, and whole milk (not part-skim) mozzarella cheese. Bake at 450°F for 10–12 minutes; makes 2 pizzas.

THE MIGHTY QUINN SERVES IT UP

JUNE 24, 2004

Watching kids as their eating habits form and solidify is not unlike witnessing a train wreck in slow motion, it's a scary and fascinating thing all at once. I'll eat anything that moves, yet my fourteen-year-old daughter, Quinn, has been a vegetarian for over two years. She decided to try it one day and never looked back. At first I was worried about her health all the time. "How can she possibly pass up a freshly grilled burger? Doesn't she want even a little bite of this Cajun-rubbed pork? Horrors, she'll have low bone density scores as an adult!" After I got tired of worrying, I got indignant. Cripe, the kid lives in a home with the food equivalent of limousine service, yet, she'd rather hitchhike.

To be fair, Quinn is not righteous or political or picky about her food, she is knowledgeable and knows that for her, eating lighter feels better. She is growing beautifully, has plenty of energy for rock climbing, and takes responsibility for her nutritional needs. I, in turn, have learned to shut-up and respect her choices.

The "vegetarian" tag may be a stretch. Technically speaking, Quinn doesn't really eat that many vegetables; she's more like a "carbatarian," an accurate but potentially inflammatory moniker in today's carb-paranoid world. We've managed to bridge our generational food gap with spinach: Quinn is willing to add fresh spinach to just about any dish. Since this is prime time for that mighty and versatile green, I thought I'd share some of her favorite food combinations. They easily fuel my busy teenager, and provide me with nice alternatives during this wonderfully warm season.

SPINACH PITA PIZZAS

Layer the following ingredients evenly among 2–whole wheat 6" pita pockets, split in half to make four flat rounds: 1–cup whole milk mozzarella cheese, shredded; ½–cup organic vegetarian pasta sauce; 1–cup fresh spinach, ribbon cut; slices of fresh garlic and bell peppers. Bake at 350°F for 6 minutes. Makes 4 pizzas.

FRESH SPINACH SALAD

Combine 4–fistfuls of fresh, clean organic spinach; ½–cup red onion, thinly sliced; 2–cups mushrooms, sliced; 2–cups fresh bean sprouts. Dressing: 2–T each of rice vinegar and sesame oil, shaken well. Toss together with clean hands, serves 2–4.

WILTED GREENS AND BOWTIE PASTA

Combine 8–ounces cooked bowtie pasta with 2–fistfuls organic spinach; 3–cloves minced garlic; ½–cup fresh Parmesan cheese; ⅓–cup olive oil. Serves 2.

TUNE INTO THE TOUR DE TASTE

JULY 8, 2004

What do you get when you combine the World Series, the Super Bowl and the finals of American Idol? For cyclists it's called the Tour de France, a bacchanalia of bikes, buff bodies, and OLN for three straight weeks in July. I love to track every grimace, crash, and scandal that erupts during this soap opera on wheels—all 2,103 miles of what is arguably the most challenging athletic event in the world.

Are you wondering what cycling has to do with food? A lot. It's a Tour of France: Burgundy's Epoisses cheese, Provence's nicoise salads, Languedoc's foie gras, profiteroles from Paris—the menu goes on for miles. The Tour riders, my heroes, push hard to end each day's stage in a new region. Tour fans have to push hard too: each evening I cook a meal and uncork a wine that salutes the cuisine of that day's stage finish. It takes a lot of stamina to eat French food every evening. (This effort, in turn, demands that I ride more often, which tends to make me hungrier, which…well, now you get the food-cycling relationship.)

There is a huge food irony at play in this event, too. When five-time winner Lance Armstrong prepares for the Tour he trains eight hours a day, he weighs his food, carefully monitoring calories. During the Tour race, these guys are riding and climbing at a brutal pace, burning up 5,000–7,000 calories a day for 21 days. These dudes are hungry. The biggest daily challenge they face is to eat enough to replace their fuel so they won't cannibalize their muscle mass. They actually get sick of eating—can you imagine such a thing? In France?!

I was curious about what these athletes actually do eat during this pedal fest, so I talked with Williston's local bike hero, retired pro Andy Bishop, who rode an amazing four Tour de France races during his career. Andy explained that riders eat all day long in the saddle from bags called "musettes." The musettes are prepared for riders by team "soigeurs" who serve as both surrogate mom and masseuse throughout the Tour. The bags contain water, Coke, small sandwiches, fruit tarts, power bars, candy and chunks of fresh pineapple, Andy's favorite item. Three hours before race time the cyclists eat big portions of spaghetti, omelets, and rice, shying away from hard-to-digest dairy products. They eat high calorie foods like muesli, meat, pasta and dessert to refuel post-ride. Then they are poured into the rack to rest, and to repeat the next day.

Yes, it's a suffer-fest, but you don't have to feel pain to be apart of the Tour de France. Over the next few weeks why not dust off your bike and go for a spin, open a French cookbook, enjoy a few fine meals, or tune into the Tour recap (evenings on channel 126) to watch sports history being made as American Lance Armstrong goes for a new world record: Tour De France victory number six. Bon Appetit!

CHOCOLATE SOUFFLÉ SALUTE

SEPTEMBER 2, 2004

In celebration of the long and luscious life of Julia Child, who died a few weeks ago, I tweaked and recorded my recipe for chocolate soufflé. Julia's wonderful cookbooks, TV shows and potent personality introduced and interpreted, for new and seasoned cooks alike, the secrets and steps of classic French cooking. This soufflé is simple and absolutely yummy served warm (or cold the next day.) It falls somewhere between a mousse, a brownie, a pudding, and a cake—what could be better? To learn more about the fundamentals of a soufflé, I suggest you read Julia's seminal book *Mastering The Art Of French Cooking.*

CHOCOLATE SOUFFLÉ SALUTE

2–t unsalted butter, room temperature, for prepping ramekins

¼–cup superfine sugar

4–T unsalted butter, room temperature

⅓–cup sugar

6–ounces best quality semisweet chocolate chips

4–eggs, separated

¼–t cream of tartar

Heat oven to 325°F. Use 2–t of butter to coat the inside of 8–four ounce ramekins. Dust with superfine sugar and tap out excess. Set them into a sheet cake pan.

In the top of a double boiler over simmering water, stir remaining butter and chocolate together until melted. Remove from heat.

In a medium bowl with an electric beater, beat egg whites and tartar until frothy. Gradually beat in sugar until mixture forms stiff peaks. Whisk egg yolks into the chocolate mixture. With a flat, wide spatula, fold one third of the egg white mixture into the chocolate. Fold in the remaining egg whites, but do not over mix.

Divide the batter among the ramekins. Place pan in the oven and gently fill it with water until it comes half way up the ramekins (this is called a bain-marie.) Bake soufflés for 20 minutes. Remove from oven and serve warm or anytime.

CREAM TOPPING

1–cup heavy cream, chilled

1–T confectioner's sugar

½–t vanilla or almond flavoring

16–fresh raspberries (optional)

Beat cream together with sugar and flavoring until stiff peaks form, top soufflés with a dollop of cream and berries.

SHARE A BOWL OF SYMPATHY

SEPTEMBER 16, 2004

This summer was tinged with a series of sad events for friends—a stroke, a bicycle accident, and a parent's death. I often found myself wondering what I could do to convey love and concern without intruding on tragedy. After trying out a million elaborate dinner ideas in my head, and then never doing a thing about it, I finally hit upon a simple gesture that I will use forever. It is heartfelt, appreciated, and easy to do for anyone you care about. A container of homemade soup, a batch of chocolate chip cookies, and a loaf of bread from a local bakery is a true godsend during times of woe.

This soup's base is a thick, dairy-free, cauliflower-potato puree that can be made into an endless array of favorite soups. When choosing the add-in ingredients I calculate "the finicky factor", considering the ages of any children who may be eating the soup. The same principle goes for the cookie recipe: keep it simple.

A nice vegetarian version combines onions, mushrooms, zucchini, chopped tomato, white beans and rosemary. For a heartier soup, add bacon, or bits of pork or chicken. Make delivery really simple for everyone by purchasing one-quart disposable containers from the deli. On the scale of things, this meal may not help very much—but it sure won't hurt, either.

CREAMY CAULIFLOWER SOUP BASE

In a soup pot combine 7–cups water or chicken stock; 1–head of cauliflower, tough center removed and chopped; 2–medium sized potatoes, peeled and chopped; 4–cloves

garlic, sliced; 1–medium onion, chopped.
Simmer uncovered for 40 minutes.

Cool slightly and then puree broth in batches. (If you prefer a chunkier version, do not puree 1–2 cups of the broth.) Season with 1–T of kosher salt and ½–t of red pepper flakes. Add additional ingredients, herbs or seasonings. To thin the soup, add a bit of water or stock. Yields 2–plus quarts of soup. Freezes well.

IN THE MOMENT AT THE MARKET

OCTOBER 14, 2004

Sure, the haunted forest is a frightening experience, but if you really want to scare yourself to death, go shopping for Halloween decorations. You'll be thoroughly spooked at the multi-season orgy going on in the aisles of your local store. Ghosts mixed with pilgrims mixed with Santa, it's three seasons on steroids, a confusing message of "hurry up and celebrate." My holiday anxiety was compounded when I picked up my mail: on the cover of an October cooking magazine sat a fat glistening roasted turkey. Enough! Don't we have forty-two days before we have to think about that meal?

This is harvest season when the freshest and best food we are going to have for a while is still available. Garden-fresh herbs, tomatoes, and late leafy greens are still delicious. Grapes, the signature food of the harvest are peak. Create your own rhythm of the seasons, attuned to the flavors and kinds of foods your palate naturally craves as the calendar gently moves you forward. Make those last bittersweet visits to the local farm stands and savor the moment, it will have to last you all winter (or at least until you start seeing the 4th of July decorations for sale!)

SIMPLE HARVEST SUPPER

This dish roasts tomatoes and grapes to create a tangy sauce that is served over individual portions of couscous. Each diner then tops off their meal with desired amounts of feta cheese, pine nuts, mint, scallions and chicken.

TOMATO GRAPE SAUCE

Preheat oven to 375°F. Toss together 3–cups of seedless red grapes; 3–cups of cherry tomatoes; 2–T olive oil; and 2–T balsamic vinegar. Place in a roasting pan and roast 45 minutes; gently turn the batch twice during the 45 minutes.

COUSCOUS

Place 3–cups of whole wheat or regular couscous in a large bowl. Pour enough boiling water over the couscous to submerge it, but don't drown it. Let it set for 5 minutes, then fluff with a chopstick.

For toppings: Toast one cup of pine nuts on a tray in the oven for 5 minutes or less—watch them carefully, they burn quickly! Crumble 1–cup of feta cheese. Thinly slice 4–scallions. Grill 4–chicken breasts; slice thinly. Chop 1–cup of fresh mint or parsley. Serves 6.

OCTOBER'S THRILLS & CHILLS

OCTOBER 28, 2004

What's the perfect meal to recover from the World Series before tackling Halloween and a Presidential election? A hot, spicy chili and melt-in-your-mouth cornbread, of course. This classic pairing is ideal to have on hand as the chill creeps in and our schedules scatter us like the final leaves falling from the trees.

My recipe has a few fun twists: a dash of maple syrup simmered with a hearty malt beer makes for a satisfying chili with rich, complex flavor—especially when it is topped with a combination of shredded sharp cheddar and Monterey jack cheeses. The cornbread is guaranteed to be moist if you use good butter and non-fat buttermilk. Both the chili and cornbread recipes double nicely and are excellent reheated in the microwave. For health purposes, avoid plastic in your microwave—always use glass containers and cover the surface with paper towel.

VERMONT STYLE CHILI

Heat a wide, deep pan on medium-high. Add 1–T of olive oil, heat thoroughly; add 1–large chopped onion and sauté for 15 minutes. Sprinkle a generous pinch of kosher salt over the cooked onion; add 1–large chopped green pepper; sauté 5 minutes more. Add 2–T minced garlic; sauté one minute. Add 1–12 ounce bottle of beer and give the pan a good stir-scrape, gathering all the browned bits from the cooking surface (this is deglazing the pan).

Add 1–pound ground beef and brown for 5 minutes. Stir in 2–16 ounce cans of kidney beans, drained, 1–28 ounce can crushed tomatoes; 2–cups beef or vegetable broth; 1–T Worcestershire sauce; ½–cup maple syrup; 1–small packet of commercial chili seasoning. Simmer uncovered for 30 minutes. Top with cheddar and Monterey Jack cheeses. Serves 6.

MELT-IN YOUR MOUTH CORNBREAD

Preheat oven to 350°F. In a bowl stir together: 1–cup corn meal; 1–cup flour; ¾–cup sugar; 4–ounces melted butter; 1–egg; 1–cup buttermilk; a dash of salt; and 2–t baking powder. Bake in a buttered glass pie plate for 22 minutes or until top cracks slightly. Serves 6.

BUILDING HOLIDAY TRADITIONS IN THE KITCHEN

NOVEMBER 25, 2004

Happy Thanksgiving! With a four-day holiday, it's time to make a fast segue into Christmas preparations while everyone is home to help out. For twenty-four years my extended family has been baking a neighborhood's worth of gingerbread houses on the day after Thanksgiving. Everyone pitches in to help: daughters, nieces, nephews, sisters and my mom. We bake 14 houses—one for each child to decorate—and a few extras to donate to favorite causes.

We do all the baking on day one. One sister is the dough expert and roller, another runs the ovens, and I am the counter; my job is to ensure that we end up with enough gingerbread sections to form14 proper houses. My mom, the conductor of our crazy cooking orchestra, runs interference, and the kids help out with everything. The next day we assemble the houses. We use a thick glue-like sugar frosting that takes a bit of skill and a lot of praying to hold the fortresses together. The houses are placed on firm pieces of cardboard (12x14") that are covered in foil. Once the houses are set (24 hours), we hold a decorating party. Long tables are set up with festive plastic tablecloths, and a ton of candy is divided into plastic cups along with individual cups of frosting and plastic knives.

When choosing candy we think "variety and volume": Lifesavers, candy canes, gummy bears, Necco wafers—you name it, we'll use it. Anything goes in the decorating department too, often what begins as a nightmare house ends up becoming the dream house. Our delivery tag reads "It is traditional to eat your gingerbread house on the first day of the New Year for good luck all year long." Good luck on this project, it's worth the effort, it's fun and a real memory maker.

GINGERBREAD HOUSE DOUGH

This recipe makes 10 houses that look small at first, but become much larger by the time the roofs are added and they are decorated. Roofs: 4.5x6.75" bake 2/house; Front and back: 5.5x4.5 in an "A" frame, bake 2/house; Sides: 2.25x6.75", bake 2 /house.

In a large bowl with an electric mixer beat together: 6–eggs; 3–cups Crisco; 3 – cups brown sugar; 3–T, each, cinnamon and ginger; 3–cups molasses, and 2–T of vinegar. Add 16.5–cups of flour and 5–T of baking soda. Mix well by hand until dough forms. Portion out two hands full of dough onto a floured work surface and roll with a pin until it is about one forth of an inch thick. Cut house sections. Repeat. Bake at 350ºF for 15 minutes on a parchment lined cookie sheet.

Frosting: Beat together 2–pounds of confectionary sugar; 1–T of white vinegar; and 3–egg whites. Keep making batches until you are done. Plan for 10–pounds of sugar and 3–dozen eggs.

STACK THE DECK WITH BREAKFAST GOODIES

DECEMBER 23, 2004

On holiday mornings it's nice to break out of the domestic routine, relax, and enjoy the celebration. Sounds like a great plan for everyone—except, of course, the person in charge of breakfast (me). It's the age-old conflict of knowing that bacon has to be fried, but I don't want to change out of my delicious new cashmere bathrobe to do it. My 2004 antidote to this dilemma is to prep a fabulous breakfast two days ahead of time, put my feet up on Christmas morning, and revel in the pandemonium. Happy holidays to all!

FALALALALA FRITTATA

A delicious quiche-like dish without all the fat and fuss.

Prep two frittatas: one is a child-pleaser with just cheese, and the second one is filled with 3–cups of special stuff like sliced avocado, shrimp, sweet peppers, tomato, herbs, spinach, and 8–ounces of shredded cheese, your choice. The rule of thumb on frittata fillings is this: if it goes well on a pizza, then it can go into the filling. Spray 2–glass pie plates with non-stick spray. Place filling ingredients in pie plates, layer cheese, wrap and store. Crack open a dozen eggs, whisk together with salt and pepper and store in a sealed container until the big day. All you have to do for breakfast is preheat the oven to 350ºF, pour half of the egg mixture into each pie plate, and bake 25 minutes. Great for reheats all day, this recipe wows 8–12 revelers.

NINA'S SOUR CREAM COFFEE CAKE

Fun to munch on during presents, this is my mom's traditional recipe

Preheat oven to 350°F. Prep a ring mold style Bundt pan with non-stick spray. In a mixer, combine the following: ¾–cup of softened butter; 1–cup sugar; 3–eggs; and 2–t almond extract. Beat for 2 minutes. Add 3–cups of flour, 1 ½–t baking powder and baking soda each; ½–t salt; and 16–ounces of non-fat sour cream. Beat until a smooth batter forms, 2–3 minutes. Spread one third of the mixture into the pan.

Filling: mix ½–cup brown sugar; 1½–t cinnamon; and ½–cup chopped walnuts (optional). Sprinkle ⅓ of the filling over batter; repeat process 2 times, end with filling on top of cake. Bake 60 minutes. Cool 10 minutes; release cake on to a cooling rack and flip. Cool; wrap in foil up to two days ahead.

Breakfast meats such as sausage and bacon can be roasted ahead in a 350°F oven for 15 – 20 minutes; wrap lightly in paper towel and store in the fridge. To reheat, simply place on a plate lined with fresh paper towel and zap in the microwave for one minute.

2005

TRY A LITTLE TENDERNESS

FEBRUARY 3, 2005

Valentine's Day is fast approaching and because I love my readers, I want you to be thinking about this day of love now. Valentine's Day is not just for lucky lovers—it's a day of affirmation and appreciation for all of the vital relationships in our lives. It's an important day because it reminds us to convey our feelings to others in word and in deed.

For my male readers this means opening up the vault of love stored in your head and heart and letting it flow out of your mouth in a way that your partner can hear, taste and feel. For example–don't just say, "I Love you, Honey"—that is the culinary equivalent of a bowl full of dog food. Sure, it's a meal, but a female cannot digest it. Try adding a little tenderness, break it down into some juicy morsels: "I Love You Honey because your eyes sparkle like diamonds and you run a chain saw better than any man I've ever met." Now, that's something a gal can sink her teeth into. (This also works well with children.)

Ladies please take note: guys are not mind readers so don't set your partners up for failure. They will not be channeling Jude Law on Valentine's Day–or any other day of the year for that matter–so give them a chance to succeed. Declare your desires! Having a conversation now about Valentine's Day (or any day, plan, or idea) and what you'd like to see happen will instantly morph you from 'bitterly disappointed pouter" to "beloved goddess". (This also works well with grumpy teens and colleagues.)

My Valentine plans? Cooking for my guy and any hungry kids that would like to join us. This is our 24th Valentine's Day together and while we've got our cha-cha-cha pretty well down, we're always seasoning the recipe of love with as much tenderizer as we can find.

TENDERLOIN FOR LOVERS

Soak 1–pound of pork tenderloin in 3–cups of apple cider mixed with 2–T of kosher salt and 1–cup soy sauce for up to 24 hours. Heat oven to 400°F. Remove tenderloin from the brine and set in a roasting pan. Roast the tenderloin for 30 minutes. Also roast 1–pound of baby red potatoes that have been tossed in olive oil and kosher salt, for 30 minutes.

While food is roasting, combine 1–cup of fresh cider with ½–cup sherry (not cooking), and 2–T of balsamic vinegar in a small saucepan. Add a handful of dried cherries or cranberries. Boil and stir sauce until thickened, about 20 minutes. Season the meat with kosher salt, fresh pepper, and a pinch of clove. Steam fresh broccolini. Serve with sliced pork, potatoes, and sauce. Serves 2–4.

THE TROJAN HORSE TEA PARTY

MARCH 3, 2005

Do your kids arrive home famished after a long day in the classroom? Mine always do. Early on I started serving dinner food right after school instead of just snacks. It's the time of day growing kids most need a serious nutrition boost to refuel for study, sports, or slumber.

I use a two-part strategy: most days a soup, casserole or local artisan bread paired with a salad (made up before the workday) are ready to go. Once a week I set up a tea party—it's a fun and creative way to regroup after a busy day. I make up a crêpe batter and start cranking the crêpes out. The girls set out the fillings: all kinds of berries, caramelized apples, sautéed bananas, Nutella, peanut butter, along with whipped cream, maple syrup, yogurt, and chopped almonds. A steaming pot of herbal tea is the perfect restorative complement.

Sounds like dessert, right? It is. There is a lot of enthusiasm for the food and the company and that is where the Trojan horse part comes in. Along with the goodies a selection of small glass bowls joins the tea time: sliced sweet peppers, cukes, broccoli florets, carrots, asparagus spears, pickles and celery sticks in some combination. The kids pick off the crunchies throughout the rest of the afternoon and evening, their sweet tooth already sated with the fruit, and then top off their tanks with a bit of pasta, cereal, or eggs that they prepare for themselves. (They can also join parents for a more elaborate dinner, or just company, later on if they wish.)

This is a great system for meeting the appetites and moods of all family members. Food is prepped in about an hour on Sunday and since the kids look forward to the teatime treat, they want to help. Crêpe batter can be made two days ahead or crêpes can be cooked ahead and stored for up to three days. Just whip together 1–egg; 1–cup of flour; 1–cup of milk, and 1–t of oil with a whisk, the batter is runny. Heat a non-stick skillet and add 2–T of batter and spread thinly; cook, flip, wait, serve.

This system creates a more relaxed buzz in the kitchen, and fewer cranky kids, but it only works if you take the time to train your children in proper kitchen protocol and safety. The kids become active participants in their food choices and develop an interest and competence in the kitchen that will last a lifetime.

It is empowering for children to have control in their lives, and you are sending the message loud and clear "you can do this!" As a bonus, you may find yourself eating a quiet meal with just your partner every once in a while. So plan ahead, share the work, and be delighted by the results.

LICKITY SPLIT ST. PATTY'S DAY PARTY

MARCH 17, 2005

The true Irish find it hysterical the way Americans celebrate St. Patrick's Day: green beer, goofy decorations, corned beef and cabbage diners. But holidays and a reason to cheer are always important—especially a holiday that falls in March when cabin fever is at pitch peak.

You can pull together a quick party by going authentic Irish: mix some Guinness Stout beer with some pale ale to whip up a traditional "Black and Tan" celebratory beverage. It is delicious and loaded with nutrients. (This is the beverage that new Irish mothers receive postpartum to restore vigor and get the breast milk flowing!) Make a pot of tea for the kids, and serve it with milk and sugar. While you are sipping on that, fry up some thick sliced bacon and preheat the oven. Mix together one of the fast Soda Bread recipes below.

Hearty and versatile soda bread can handle anything you might like to serve, from butter and jam, to flowing egg yolks, to dense pates—it's fabulous and easy! This bread is great all by itself, too; I'm thinking it must have inspired the old Irish proverb "I don't even butter my bread, I consider that cooking." So keep it simple and authentic, and *Erin Go Braugh*!

TRADITIONAL IRISH SODA BREAD

Preheat oven to 375°F. Combine 3 ½–cups of flour with ½–t each of sugar; salt; and baking soda. With clean hands, knead in 2–cups of buttermilk (or fresh milk spiked with 1–T of vinegar.) You can add 1–cup of raisins and/or 2–T of caraway seeds if you like. The dough will be sticky, so carefully mold it into a mound and place on a baking sheet dusted with cornmeal. Score it with an "X" in the top of the dough and bake for 35 minutes or until it sounds hollow when tapped on the bottom.

IRISH BROWN SODA BREAD

Follow the same directions above, except combine 2–cups of whole-wheat flour with 1–cup white flour and ½–cup oatmeal flakes; then add remaining dry ingredients. Omit raisins and caraway seeds.

WINE TASTING 101

MAY 12, 2005

Wine is a hobby at our house, but over the years I think we've forgotten way more than we actually know about it. Just when we've hit the age when we can afford some of the good stuff, our eroding memory banks fail to keep up with the details and complexities of such a vast subject. Yet we're always excited about expanding our knowledge and enjoyment of wine, so we teamed up with another couple to create some momentum. We've hit upon a fun tasting formula that keeps us focused on the wine and the learning curve high, but without getting too stuffy or serious about it all.

Four times a year each host couple invites one guest couple, for a total of eight tasters per session. At each tasting, serious wines are sampled in three flights poured among 24 identical globe glasses (8 champagne glasses and 8 dessert wine glasses round out our portable "wine kit".) Discussion floats among wine related topics: region, grape, winemaker, travel experiences, vintage or any other tidbits we can contribute. When I say serious wines, I don't mean pricey. We do our homework by befriending local wine sellers, and we've had consistent winners within the $6–$25 range. We don't taste the wine blind, but we do keep the price tag quiet until everyone has had a chance to share their impressions. We love it when an inexpensive wine steals the show, like the "little vixen" from Argentina, Vila Tinto Fundacion, that seduced everyone way before we learned of the her $5.99 price tag.

We begin the evening gathered around the kitchen island with a sparkling wine, complemented by an array of nuts, olives, and cheeses. Then we move on to three flights of graduated sophistication: red or white chosen by grape, geography or even a theme (we once did wines with animal labels—a disaster!) A few platters of protein-rich hors d'oeuvres are served tapas style, and we finish strong with a seated dessert, coffee, and a dessert wine.

This is an easy event to execute. One host selects the wine: 1–bottle of sparkling, 2–bottles for each of 3 flights, 1–dessert wine. Guests bring hors d'oeuvres, and a host makes or buys dessert. The host couples split the wine bill (it's cheaper and a lot more fun than a dinner party!)

Once a year we have an "alumni bash" for all the tasters to meet each other and compare notes. And each year our reunion party gets bigger and better as we have fun jogging each other's memories to become better informed about wine.

THE LITTLE RED HEN LOSES IT

JUNE 23, 2005

Every hard-working cook knows that the real satisfaction from cooking must be intrinsic. Who else in their right mind would spend hours learning recipes, planning meals, writing up shopping lists, driving to the supermarket to walk aisle after aisle to load up a giant cart with food, and then unload it on to a conveyor belt? Then scan the food, pay for it with coupons, pack it into plastic, load it back into the giant cart, roll it out the parking lot to reload into the trunk, drive it home, unload it again from the car, unpack it in the kitchen, stock it, and then remove it again from shelves to prep it, cook it, serve it, and clean up the mess?

After twenty-two years of this food marathon it is just dawning on me that NO ONE in my family dares to acknowledge the existence of this insane drill; they realize that if they offer to pitch in I might wake up to the ridiculous rigor of this ritual and call the whole thing off. An occasional "kiss the cook" peck on the cheek is the only recognition they dare dole out. I am their grocery automaton and they like it this way.

Thank goodness that at midlife Mother Nature steps in and does some special favors for women like me. For example, last night I went to bed after a late evening food excursion and had the most wonderful nightmare. I dreamt that I was wielding a broom handle like an AK47 down the cereal aisle screaming "Little red hen no more, little red hen no more" as I wiped out row after row of boxes containing sugar-coated crap.

Next, I found myself on a bobcat in the snack aisle happily excavating the entire chip inventory with a crunch that set off an earthquake, which in turn tumbled the million bottles of juice choices off their shelves and created a giant sticky pool for all of the fish and beef and chicken to swim together in.

Flour was everywhere as I tossed five-pound bags around in a pillow fight with the eggs in the dairy case. The only section that went unscathed was the chocolate aisle; it was a delicious dream.

When I woke up I had a smile on my face and a great idea. School's out for summer, I've got kids who drive. You won't see me in the grocery store until fall.

JUST FOR THE HALIBUT

JULY 7, 2005

In my last column, "The Little Red Hen Loses It", the labors of schlepping food struck quite a nerve with my loyal readers, so here's a brief update about how *not* shopping's been going. I haven't technically shopped at a supermarket for three weeks now, and... I'm loving it!

I did tiptoe into Shaw's today, just to get my supersaver coupon validated before the deadline, so if you saw me there–I swear–I was not shopping! And to all of you that I bumped into at Costco the other day with my orange boat loaded with booty, I contend that this is a different topic altogether, for a Costco trip is the cook's equivalent of a day at Disney.

I'll admit that I did stop into Adam's wonderful farm market yesterday, but just for their native strawberries, it being the season and all. But when I saw their homegrown basil and red leaf lettuces I started to panic at what I might miss, so I grabbed a handful, plus some tomatoes, melon and a baguette, too, just for the hell of it.

So far my summer shoppers, daughters #1 and #2, have performed on a scale ranging from abysmal to very fine. Shopper #1 has been at bat twice: week one she came home with a bill for $140.00 of which $64.50 was for health and beauty aids: hair dye, paste on nails, shaving cream for women only, etc. Actual food included Lucky Charms, Triscuits, Oreos, grape tomatoes, and a package of chicken. After I got done gnawing on my arm, we had a meeting and wrote a more detailed list for the following week; her batting average went up by 900%.

Shopper #2 worked well off the list, and then did some improvising, which is where the fun began. Among other goodies, she bought 2–pounds of halibut and some Montreal-style frozen bagels, two items I'd never purchased. I felt just like the Iron Chef cooking with these random ingredients, and the happy result is a divine halibut dish dripping in golden bagel crumbs. So far I'd say this shopping experiment has been worthwhile, even if it's just for the halibut.

LEMON ROASTED HALIBUT

Preheat oven to 425°F. Remove the zest from a lemon, cut in half, and squeeze juice over the bottom of a roasting pan. Lay 2–pounds of halibut into pan, do not overlap; squeeze the remaining lemon juice and sprinkle with kosher salt. Toast 3 Montreal-style bagels, let cool. Place lemon zest and 3–garlic cloves in a food processor, process 60 seconds; add bagels and pulse lightly until chunks form. Add 2–T of cold butter and pulse 30 seconds until coarse crumbs form. Top halibut with crumbs, packing gently. Roast in a hot oven for 18–20 minutes. Serves 4–6.

CHILLIN' WITH MOM'S SUMMER SOUP

JULY 21, 2005

It's July, and everyday Mother Nature's vegetable world is erupting in a delicious riot of colors, flavors and textures. The produce available now is epic, and nothing showcases it better than my Mom's gazpacho.

Gazpacho gahz-PAH-choh) is a tomato-based soup of chopped vegetables served ice cold. It refreshes and restores like nothing else during the dog days of summer. The soup is a wonderful base for any style of meal: usually Mom serves it with a simple dollop of crème fraiche or sour cream, but for special evenings there might be a precious lump of lobster tail or some shrimp swimming among the veggies.

When Mom serves the soup for comfort food on a steamy, rainy day, golden homemade croutons, pan toasted in good olive oil, bob invitingly on top. The variations for gazpacho garnishes are infinite, have your way with it! I love this soup because it embodies all that my Mother taught me about cooking: fresh is best, less is more, and a good bowl of soup will do more for world peace than any political soapbox. Thanks, Mom, and pots full of love!

PAT MYETTE'S SUMMER GAZPACHO

In a large prep bowl combine 3–large local tomatoes, chopped, seeds and all. Add 1–chopped cucumber; 1–chopped green pepper; 1–cup chopped celery, and ½–cup chopped scallions. Add 2–ripe avocados, peeled and chopped.

Stir in 4–cups V8 juice; ¼–cup red wine vinegar; ¼–cup olive oil; kosher salt to taste; ½–t white pepper; 3–cloves garlic, minced; 2–T fresh lemon juice; ½–t Tabasco sauce (optional).Cover and chill overnight. This recipe is a chunky textured version; all of the vegetables may be pureed if you prefer a smoother finished product. Yields 2 quarts, plus.

THE COFFEE DECK

AUGUST 4, 2005

There's this place in my life called the coffee deck. It sits attached to the back of a charming lakeside cottage on Lake Memphremagog, three miles from the Canadian border. Facing east to welcome the morning sun, my haven of wood is a dozen feet long, half as wide, and painted one of the thousand shades of green bursting in Vermont's Northeast Kingdom.

From my deck I watch the sunrise over Brigham Hill, eavesdropping on busy birds chatting with their neighbors, and I am filled with the desire for some early morning conversation, too. I meet my mom on the deck where two old fashioned metal chairs, surprisingly sturdy and comfortable, welcome the early risers. The chairs bounce a little as I sit, waking up my sleepy bones, stirring my body gently into conversation over hot coffee splashed with cream. It's simple stuff like "how did you sleep last night?" and "isn't it a gorgeous morning?" Slowly shooting the breeze with a live person—nothing heavy, nothing profound, just quiet conversation to welcome the day.

Last week I sat with mom on the coffee deck and we sipped steaming Dominican coffee, nibbled on sugar crullers. It was a blissful morning, my only one on a blitz-visit as teenagers experimented with holding down the fort down at home. They are old enough to stay alone, but not old enough for me to relax about it, so my cell phone was there to cushion concern.

As mom and I chatted, my phone rang, ordering me to answer it. I am ashamed to admit it, but I did answer it—and more than once. With one fell swoop of technology I eclipsed years of a timeless, dignified ritual—quiet conversation on the coffee deck. I was caught squarely in a breech between courtesy and convenience and I am sad to say that technology won that round.

Rude? Reactive? Ridiculous? Guilty on all counts, but I wish I could say my faux pas was an aberration. Ubiquitous intruders, our cellular "lifelines" threaten to strangle the very throats that give voice to that which keeps us all truly connected: quiet conversations over a hot cup of coffee.

MAKE A DATE WITH GREAT INGREDIENTS

AUGUST 18, 2005

The matchmaker in me is always trying to pair foods for eternal bliss at the table. Now that local tomatoes have arrived, it's raining men, and I'm in a frenzy to introduce them to my kitchen friends: olive oil, kosher salt, basil, garlic and vodka.

At no other time of the year will tomatoes be fresher or easier to prepare, so start off by making a date to visit a farmer's market or farm stand in your area—the tomatoes should be firm, rosy, and not too handsome. Bring them home and employ the "less is more" technique: a little kosher salt, a dash of best quality olive oil, maybe some herbs, and *voila*—wedding bells will be ringing.

Last night I put a cast iron pan on a hot grill, added some olive oil, and seared fresh tuna; as it cooked, I cut up a few tomatoes and sprinkled them with kosher salt. While the tomatoes waited for the tuna, I gently hand mixed some baby greens with just a dash each of lemon juice and olive oil. The kosher salt mingled with the tomato juices to release the full power of their flavor; the combination of the fresh food and simple technique was simply a match made in heaven.

In the bounty of the next few weeks we'll be speed-dating tomatoes, and that will include whipping up a tomato-based sauce. At this point in the relationship, we can introduce vodka to tomatoes. Sounds like a potential mismatch, but Woody Allen will argue there's no such thing. When vodka is added to tomatoes it stimulates the release of flavors that water or fats cannot. In cooking, alcohol is kind of gender-confused and acts a little like fat and a little like water. Also, vodka doesn't have any flavor of its own to impart, so we get an intensely concentrated tomato flavor. (And you thought Bove's Vodka Sauce was just sexy marketing!)

A SAUCE TO REMEMBER

Roughly chop 6–tomatoes, seeds, skin and all. Place in a saucepan heated with 2–T of olive oil. Add 1–T of vodka, 1–T freshly minced garlic, and a dash of kosher salt. Simmer lightly for 5–10 minutes and serve over pasta; top with fresh basil leaves. Serves 2–4.

THE COOK GETS A GRILLING

SEPTEMBER 1, 2005

Have you ever enjoyed a dish at a party and quizzed the cook on how it was prepared? A generous cook will share enthusiastically—but here's a warning: they may be guilty of omission of facts. Cooks tend to be light on detail because basic knowledge or steps are so ingrained they don't really think about it. I was guilty of this recently at a family party for my mom's 70th birthday.

I had grilled a large platter of fresh veggies for dinner: Roma tomatoes, yellow and green squash, peppers, red onion, eggplant, and cauliflower. I thought it was a simple execution of the season's finest, no big deal. That is, until my sister, who has a palate like Jean-Georges Vongerichten, put me on the cook's witness stand and started grilling me for the details.

She loves to entertain and I could see where this platter might end up on her weekend menu. "What did you do to make these veggies so good?" she asked. "I just grilled them in a little oil." "What kind of oil" she wanted to know. "Umm….olive oil?" "No, no, I can see that the veggies are fit for a photo shoot, and I can also taste rosemary, thyme, and tarragon." "Wow, she's good," I thought, "Why didn't she become a lawyer?"

Here I was sincerely thinking that my technique had been "just a little olive oil" when in reality, there was way more detail to it than that. I had actually used grape seed oil to baste the vegetables. It has a light, delicate taste and a high smoke point (485°F) that permits high heat cooking without smoking the food gray. The grape seed oil preserves the color and integrity of the vegetables, and the grill marks are awesome. This particular can of oil was infused with a delightful mixture of Herbs de Provence, something I hadn't really paid attention to, but it elevated the vegetables to a new level of flavor.

Grapeseed oil is one of the healthiest cooking oils. It raises the good cholesterol (HDL) and lowers the bad stuff (LDL). It has no cholesterol, no sodium, and only about half of the saturated fat of olive oil. It is sold in the oil or health food sections of markets, but I found my 30–ounce can at Marshall's for $7.99. Now that testimony is in, here's the verdict: grape seed oil is worth its' weight in gold!

A MODERN DAY POMPEII

SEPTEMBER 15, 2005

Many years ago I visited Pompeii, Italy, where Mt. Vesuvius erupted on August 23, 79 AD; it wiped out a region and created "the forgotten city". Inhabitants perished as powerful surges of steaming gas and ash burned and suffocated their lungs. The ash buried the bodies, and the particles fused in a natural weathering process. As the corpses decayed, they left spooky shaped voids in the ash. It took 1500 years for archaeologists to find the forgotten city and learn about the fate of the citizens of Pompeii.

Almost to the day, one thousand nine hundred and twenty six years later, another city and region was wiped out by powerful surges of hurricane water that burned and suffocated their lungs and buried people in watery graves. As the bodies decayed, they bloated and floated along spooky main streets. It took the modern equivalent of 1500 years for authorities to find this forgotten city and learn about the fate of the citizens of New Orleans.

What is striking about Pompeii is how perfectly a moment in time is preserved—the decayed bodies, now reconstructed in plaster of Paris, pose in a montage of daily life. It's a freeze frame that tells us so much about them: water was scare and hauled often, couch-like banquettes encouraged intensive socializing over meals, and in the kitchen, pots on a stone counter still sit today, inviting visitors to peek at what's for dinner. The people of Pompeii knew trouble was coming that day, and they died performing their daily rituals.

The hurricane victims of the south were like-minded. They knew danger was brewing, but they stuck to their rhythms, not quite believing that a storm could possibly wreak such havoc. In the aftermath of disaster, survivors who still had the remnants of a home maintained ritual. Neighbors in the French Quarter banded together to haul water from stores, they socialized intensely, and gave each other spritz baths of bleach, water and comfort. They grilled decaying food, and served every meal with warm white wine and a toast.

Human rituals are vital to survival, they keep us sane and focused; while strong enough for disasters, they are even more powerful when we control our own fate. We cannot reverse the tragic misfortunes of our southern neighbors, but we can honor their struggles by truly appreciating the history of our own good fortune.

Taking a moment to savor the importance of our own kitchen rituals when preparing food; feasting on a chunk of gratitude for the dry, safe kitchen, running water, and humming refrigerator; sharing an extra scoop of affection for the family members who are present for the meal.

DO YOU KNOW THE MUFFIN MAN?

OCTOBER 5, 2005

Convincing a child to eat a nutritious breakfast can be as difficult as coaxing them out of bed on a cold school morning. And while PopTarts may be touted as a good recovery food for athletes, they simply don't cut it for kids as a meal. Children need complex combinations of sugar, starch, protein and fat to sustain their energy throughout the morning and to boost their ability to learn. A balanced breakfast fuels children with energy and prevents a drop in blood sugar for several hours. A bowl of oatmeal and milk sprinkled with blueberries and maple syrup, or an egg on a whole wheat English muffin with some orange juice does the trick nicely.

Children who skip breakfast are two times more likely to be overweight; studies have proven a direct link between regular breakfast consumption and lower body mass. Breakfast eaters may eat more calories per day, but they are less likely to struggle with weight issues—tell that to your dieting teenager. With obesity at an all time high in the United States, breakfast seems like a good place to begin the battle for health.

I won't fib and say my girls never eat PopTarts on the run, but I've found it is possible to have quick and healthy breakfast foods available most mornings. Some suggestions: melon, grapes, strawberries, apples, or mango cut into chunks—it's amazing what kids will eat when they can use toothpicks.

For fruit smoothies blend canned pineapple and a ripe banana with 1–cup of yogurt, 1–cup of orange juice and some ice to make a really nice treat. Add 1–cup of soft tofu to boost protein (they'll never know what's in it.) For sandwiches smother some whole wheat bread with unprocessed peanut butter, a sliced banana and honey—then grill it. With a glass of milk on the side, this is breakfast nirvana. For kids on the run, try whipping up nutritious and delicious muffins, they stay moist for days and freeze well.

MORNING RUSH MUFFINS

Preheat oven to 375ºF. In a mixing bowl stir together 3–cups Raisin Bran Cereal; 1–cup buttermilk; 3–T canola oil; 2–eggs; ¼–cup light brown sugar; ¼–cup molasses; 1–ripe smashed banana. Let batter rest for 5 minutes. Gently stir in 1–cup whole wheat flour and 1–t baking soda. Fill 12 prepared muffin tins. Divide 1–cup blueberries, or raspberries, or chopped apple among the muffins using a chop stick to gently incorporate. Top with a sprinkle of oats and nuts. Bake 20 minutes.

COOKIES MAKE THE WORLD GO 'ROUND

OCTOBER 13, 2005

Ever feel like you could be a potential victim of the C.O.O.K.I.E. syndrome? (Yup, look in the mirror: Crazed, Overloaded, Obsessive Keeping It Extreme.) In our techno-charged world, stress accumulates at a frightening rate; rarely is there a convenient time to diffuse backlogged tensions. My Cookie Stress Management Program is a great method for releasing stress each day. There are four simple steps to follow: 1. Breathe deeply for a minute or two 2. Drink a glass of water 3. Go for a short walk 4. Eat one really good homemade cookie. I think cookies are the food equivalent of a child's blankie—they make me feel safe, comforted, and brave.

Cookies have a timeless, celebrity appeal, too—just like Oprah. They have the unabashed confidence to break down barriers, telegraph warmth, and promote good feelings (like world peace.) The other day I really messed up a park & ride rendezvous with my biking group. When we finally hit the road I was contrite, yet we traveled in stony silence. When I couldn't stand it any longer, I extracted a bag of homemade Green Mountain Double Chocolate Chip Chews from my backpack for some group therapy. The tension instantly evaporated, everybody relaxed, and our usual friendly banter began to flow. I'll tell you, mea culpa never tasted so good.

MASTER COOKIE DOUGH RECIPE

Preheat oven to 350°F. Bake cookies for 12–14 minutes.

In a large bowl beat with a mixer: 1–pound soft unsalted butter, 1½–cups brown sugar; and 1–

cup white sugar, until fluffy. Beat in 4–eggs; 4–t of vanilla; 2–t baking soda; and 2–t of baking powder. Switch to a wooden spoon and stir in 2–cups of coconut, then 5–cups white flour.

GREEN MOUNTAIN DOUBLE CHOCOLATE CHIP CHEWS

To the master dough recipe stir in 3–cups of rolled oats; 8–cups of chocolate chips; and 2–cups chopped pecans.

UNFORGETTABLE OATMEAL CHEWS

To the master dough recipe stir in 6–cups of rolled oats; 3–cups of raisins; and 2–cups chopped walnuts.

A BITTER-SWEET SEASON

OCTOBER 27, 2005

A huge wall of bittersweet vine cascades into my garden like a waterfall. The yellow and green leaves mingle brilliantly with the orange berries to signal the turn of another Vermont season. The bittersweet vine is an eloquent symbol of how I feel about this time of year, about this time of life. I hate to see the days getting shorter and colder, yet I love to ski. I miss my children going away to school, yet I am pleased for their progress. I'm heartbroken to see my darling eighty-five-year-old mother-in-law ill and fading, yet I know she has led a remarkable life.

The palate signals the stomach during this season of change, too, demanding more aromatic contrasts. Food needs to be a little heartier, the flavors a bit more intense. I cooked this autumn-themed meal for my extended family last week; the menu was a nice bridge into cold weather eating—the food filled our bellies with what we craved while it comforted our bittersweet hearts.

SWEET AND TART RED CABBAGE

Heat oven to 400°F. In a large ovenproof casserole, melt 4–ounces of butter on medium-hi heat. Add 1–large onion, finely chopped; 2–cloves of minced garlic; 3–T of sugar and simmer for 5 minutes. Add 1–cup vegetable stock, ½–cup red wine, ¼–cup honey, and 4–T red wine vinegar. Add 1–medium head of thinly sliced red cabbage (10–cups). Combine well and braise in oven for 45–60 minutes. Serves 6.

PORK TENDERLOIN WITH SPICY FIG SAUCE

Dry and salt 2–1 pound (plus) pork tenderloins with some kosher salt. Heat ¼–cup olive oil on med-high in an ovenproof pan. Sear the pork, turning on each of the four sides with tongs until meat is nicely browned, about 2 minutes per side. Sprinkle in some baby red potatoes, cut in half, around the meat and place the pan in a 400°F oven to roast for 25 minutes. Remove and tent with foil for 10 minutes. Slice meat and serve with Fig Sauce; serves 6.

Fig Sauce: Heat an 8–ounce jar of fig preserves in the microwave for 45 seconds on hi. Carefully pour contents into a mixing bowl and add 2–T of Dijon mustard; 2–T of soy sauce; 4–minced garlic cloves; and ½–t of red pepper flakes. Whisk and adjust for taste using small increments of brown sugar and pepper: the sauce should be sweet and hot. Simmer sauce 10 minutes; serve over sliced pork.

ALL TECHED-OUT AND NOWHERE TO GO

NOVEMBER 10, 2005

I'm exhausted. I've spent the past six weeks launching my new writing website kimdannies.com and I'm melted into a mass of microchips from all of the nerve wracking detail that such an endeavor demands. I thought the web would simplify my writing life—what a laugh! My brain is fried from choosing images, fonts, and meta-tags, and I'm too tired to write. Google this, download that—if the ipower tech support company put me on hold one more time, my phone would have been found pulsed to shreds in the Cuisinart. Thank heaven for my wonderful web designer, Mary Hill, who kept me sane and moving forward; she even created a special section just for my Everyday Gourmet readers to visit archived recipes and discover new food stories (click on "writing" from home page.)

I feel like I've delivered a baby—all I want to do is lay on the couch and sip some of my garlic potato soup laced with sherry and cream. Maybe if I can figure out how to turn on my DVD player (without experiencing another tech-induced nervous breakdown) I'll relax for a bit with my new favorite movie "What's Cookin?" It's a hilarious parody about families coming together at Thanksgiving and communicating the old fashioned way: talking face to face.

CREAMY GARLIC POTATO SOUP

Peel 6–medium potatoes and cut into quarters. Place in a cooking pot and just barley cover the potatoes with cold water. Add 6–whole garlic cloves and 1–medium chopped onion. Cover and bring to a full boil on high heat, then simmer the soup for 20 minutes until potatoes are very soft. Warm 1 ½–cups of milk with 2–T of sherry; and 2–T of butter in the microwave, on hi, for 1–minute. Mash the potatoes and add milk mixture. With an electric beater, whip the soup until it is smooth. Adjust the flavor with kosher salt and white pepper. Serve warm with a dollop of crème fraiche. Serves 6.

A RECIPE FOR HOLIDAY SUCCESS

NOVEMBER 24, 2005

Would you like a recipe for a wonderful family celebration? A good rule of thumb is to keep the heart a little softer than the head, the hands a little busier than the mouth, and your smile a little more generous than your waistline. Contribute to the event and focus on the things you are thankful for; ignore grandpa's criticism of your teenager's hairdo, or that cousin who locked you in the trunk as a child. To further diffuse stress, be in the moment. Absolutely *do not* permit any discussion of the Christmas menu during Thanksgiving (my family does this!)

Cocktail–time can often be a prelude to a family feud. Make sure to have raw vegetables, fun non-alcoholic beverages, and other healthy alternatives to the heavy hors d'oeuvres usually served during cocktail hour. Please don't make guests wait for hours to eat, serve the meal within ninety minutes and then let people relax on their own schedule. It's a good idea to pace the feast a bit. After the meal, clean up, and then take a walk; serve dessert during the football game.

When it comes to clean-up time, don't buy the "I'm sleepy from the tryptophan in turkey" excuse from slackers. They'll have to find another reason for feeling too tired to help out with the post meal clean-up. L–tryptophan doesn't act on the brain unless you take it on an empty stomach with no protein present. The levels found in a turkey dinner are far too low to have such an effect. So, even though the media blame post holiday meal sleepiness on the turkey dinner, it's just flashy PR, not food fact.

It's more likely due to the combination of drinking alcohol (remember Seinfeld's wine-in–the-box and turkey episode?), social stress, and overeating. Eating turkey combined with the mashed potato-creamed onion-cranberry sauce-sweet potato-stuffing-bread-pie-whipped cream onslaught draws blood away from the brain to aid in the digestive tract's massive job.

That's why it's important not to hold grudges during this holiday, it's bad for digestion: swallow your pride and get on with the celebration. A Happy and healthy Thanksgiving to all!

"OLIVE," THE OTHER REINDEER

DECEMBER 22, 2005

Is your kitchen beginning to buzz with hungry people seeking traditional holiday treats? I love chaos in the kitchen at Christmas and the food memories it sparks—it is the stuff of family legend. One of ours started in 1995 when, on the smug authority of a 5–year old, our Quinn announced that "Olive" was Santa's ninth reindeer (the one who used and laugh and call Rudolph names.) Pandemonium erupted as her big sisters shrieked and ran through the kitchen in disbelief that she could be so dumb. I was in awe that Quinn had come up with such an astute observation; it was one of those mother's moments I never want to forget. To help me preserve that precious memory I make the olive spread, Tapenade, every single holiday season.

Tapenade (TA-puh-nahd) is a thick paste made from pitted olives, capers, anchovies, olive oil and garlic. (If you don't like anchovies or capers leave them out, you'll love the results anyway.) Tapenade can be made from green or black olives and is fabulous spread simply on a piece of toasted baguette. It really shines when dolloped over grilled meats, fish, or pasta and veggies, for a quick dinner sauce.

I recently saw a cool hors d'oeuvre tray featuring tiny pools of Tapenade perched on slices of peeled English cucumber and half slices of hard boiled eggs—it was a beautiful and refreshing presentation, not to mention easy and healthful. For a memorable lunch, smear it on great bread for a cold meat sandwich of salami or prosciutto paired with greens and tomato slices.

I used to pit my own olives for Tapenade, which was a pain, but now it is so easy with the wonderful selection of pitted olives at the supermarket olive station. One 16–ounce container will yield a cup of Tapenade. Because it is rich, it goes far. And beware, this stuff with a nice glass of wine may create pandemonium in your kitchen, it's that good.

As we gather our extended families together this week to get reacquainted, to bump and jostle in the kitchen, and to create new food memories, remember the legend of Olive—for she is the spirit of the holidays, and she is everywhere.

TAPENADE

In a food processor combine a 16–ounce container of pitted green or black olives, 2–T of capers; 2–T of extra virgin olive oil; 4–garlic cloves; and 4–slivers of canned anchovy. Pulse the mixture until a rough paste forms. (Add more olive oil for smoother paste.) Season the paste with kosher salt and freshly ground pepper, to taste. Store in the fridge covered, use within 3 days. Yields 1 ½–cups.

2006

COOKING UP A BREAK

FEBRUARY 23, 2006

Cook up some fun in the kitchen during the school mid-winter break. Start by surprising your kids with a feast of crêpes served with fresh berries and whipped cream for breakfast. They'll love chocolate Nutella, peanut butter, sliced apples or applesauce, bananas, and maple syrup on them, too.

For lunch, how about a grilled peanut butter, honey and banana sandwich? Kids can customize their creation by adding chocolate chips or potato chips for extra crunch and giggles. Lightly butter 2 whole-wheat slices of bread per child and place face down on a hot grill. Spread peanut butter, drizzle honey, and add sliced bananas on one slice. Top with the other slice when it is nicely browned. This yummy sandwich will ooze with flavor and is perfect with a glass of cold milk and baby carrots.

For the evening meal there is nothing more fun to make for dinner than homemade pasta. Making the pasta dough is easy. Wash little hands, and then set each child up at their own station with a medium sized bowl. Into each bowl add 1–cup of flour. Next, have your chefs make a "well" in the center of the flour by pushing it back to create an opening the size of a tennis ball. Into the well add 1–egg yolk (save the whites for macaroons), 1–t of salt; 1–T of olive oil; and 1–T of water. Let the kids gently mix the ingredients by hand to form dough. You may need to add a bit more water or flour to achieve this goal. When dough is formed, collect separate balls on a parchment lined cookie sheet and get everyone cleaned up.

Next, set up the pasta machine up and start cranking. The gluten in the flour must be worked so each section of dough passes through the press 6–8 times with gradually more pressure. This is achieved by setting the rollers closer together every third time the dough passes through. Kids love the repetition of this process and become expert at it quickly. Just remember to dust the dough with a bit of flour and fold it in half each time it goes through until about the seventh time. At this stage let it pass through a tight roller for a final stretch and layer each section of dough separated by a piece of plastic wrap.

Decide on the cut setting for the pasta, I think fettuccini cooks up best. Start cutting–it takes two people–and place cut pasta on the backs of chairs or over a balanced yardstick to dry. Fill a large wide mouthed pot with water and boil. Add pasta and cook 3 minutes, it will rise in the pot when it's ready. Serve it with butter and kosher salt or your child's favorite sauce. Be sure to save some of the pasta for a quiet dinner for yourself, later, when your little gourmets have gone to bed.

CUCKOO FOR QUINN'S COCONUT CAKE

MARCH 9, 2006

This splendid cake is a family favorite for Quinn's March birthday. We first spotted it on the cover of a *Southern Living* magazine in 1995, and went on to adapt the recipe to our own northern ways of cooking. Although it seems sophisticated, it is easy to make and teaches a few new techniques. We love this cake because it celebrates change—growing a year older and the change of seasons. The fluffy white frosting reminds us of the final snowstorm of winter, while the lemon curd hints that spring is not too far away.

YELLOW CAKE

Preheat the oven to 350°F and spray 3–9" round cake pans with non-stick spray.

In a mixing bowl combine 1–18.25 ounce package of yellow cake mix with 1 ⅓–cups of water; 3–eggs; ½–cup canola oil; and 1–t of vanilla.

Mix well and divide batter among the three pans. Bake 15–18 minutes until tester comes out clean. Cool cakes for 10 minutes then invert onto cooling racks.

LEMON CURD FILLING

Combine 1–cup of sugar with ¼–cup cornstarch in a medium saucepan. Stir in 1–cup of boiling water and cook over medium heat, stirring constantly, until sugar and cornstarch dissolve (2–4 minutes.)

Crack 4–egg yolks into a small mixing bowl. Reserve the whites for the frosting recipe below.

Gradually stir about ¼ of the hot mixture into the yolks. Add yolk mixture back into the sugar water, stirring constantly with a whisk. Stir in ⅓–cup fresh lemon juice and cook until thickened, about a minute. Whisk in 2–T of butter. Let curd cool and thicken.

FLUFFY WHITE FROSTING

In a medium sized saucepan combine 1–cup sugar; 1 ½–cups of water; and 2–T of corn syrup. Cook, without stirring, until mixture reaches the 'soft ball' stage or 240ºF on a candy thermometer. This can take up to 30 minutes and the consistency will be syrup-like.

Beat 4–reserved egg whites and ¼–t cream of tartar at high speed with an electric mixer until soft peaks form. Slowly add sugar syrup, beating constantly until stiff peaks form and frosting is desired consistency.

TO ASSEMBLE

Place first layer of cake on a footed cake plate. Spread half of lemon curd on top of the cake face. Add second tier of cake on top of it. Spread remainder of lemon curd, then add third tier. Frost cake with fluffy frosting then cover entire cake with sweetened coconut flakes.

MAC & CHEESE: IT'S HOT!

APRIL 6, 2006

Mac & Cheese is a lot like blue jeans: dress it up, or dumb it down, and it's always right, always hot. Is there a more comfortably indulgent dish on the planet?

Ask my friend who had the misfortune of lunching with me. She innocently ordered SmokeJack's Mac & Cheese studded with Apple Bacon for lunch. There was a group mugging when it arrived. Pathetic salad-and-fish refugees, we mooned like the family dog until we were graciously invited to attack her plate at will. Next time I'm ordering the Mac & Cheese outright.

In the meantime, I'm putting it on the menu for our family's annual Spring Brunch. I'm thinking that if there is enough of something great to go around people will be happy right off the bat, and maybe even mind their manners. I'll spruce up my standard with signs of spring: asparagus, Vidalia onion, spicy ham, and early spinach. A bubbling breadcrumb topping will transform into it something gorgeous. Brunch is at 10; and yes, wear your blue jeans.

SPRING MAC & CHEESE SPLURGE

This recipe does not double well, so make two batches if necessary. 1 pound of bow tie pasta in a 9x12" baking dish is a good fit.

Preheat oven to 375°F. Boil 1–pound of bow tie pasta for 8 minutes; drain. Place in prepped baking dish.

Béchamel Sauce: over medium heat in a large sauté pan, melt 2–T of butter. Whisk in ¼–cup of flour. Thick clumps will appear so keep it moving in the pan by slowly whisking in ½–cup of milk. A smooth sauce will form.

Whisk in 1–cup of milk; 1–cup of cream; and 2–T of Dijon mustard; heat until barely bubbling. Stir in 4–chopped garlic cloves; 2–cups chopped onion; 2–large pinches kosher salt; and 1–t red pepper flakes.

Whisk in 6–ounces of shredded cheddar and fontina cheeses, each; warm through. Add 2–cups chopped asparagus; 1–cup cubed ham; and 1–cup shredded fresh spinach. Pour mixture over the pasta, cover with foil, and bake for 20 minutes.

Place 4–garlic cloves in a food processor; chop. Add 3–thick slices of bread from a loaf of multigrain, pulse on/off for 15 seconds. Add 2–T of cold butter. Pulse on/off for 30 seconds. When Mac & Cheese has baked for 20 minutes, remove foil and place breadcrumbs all over surface of pasta. Bake 10–12 minutes until dish is bubbling and browned. Serves 6.

TURNING OVER A NEW LEAF

APRIL 20, 2006

No secret about it, we're having a bona fide spring in Vermont this year—a miracle for marveling. With everything turning green and sprouting like crazy, I feel just like Mary Lennox running around the grounds of Misselthwaite Manor shouting, "It's wick, it's wick!"

I even bought my lettuce seeds for two large window box containers that sit on my deck. All season I'll be growing gorgeous varieties of greens that don't need to be washed or weeded. To keep it coming, I'll reseed the boxes every few weeks. Butterhead bib, little Caesar, Ruby, Grand Rapids, a Looseleaf blend of Blackseeded Simpson, Deer Tongue, Green Ice, Lolla Rossa and Mighty Red Oak will mix and mingle with sweet basil and chives to round out my salad garden. Since I'm more of a yardener than a gardener, it's a simple but rewarding way to enjoy the bounty of Vermont's growing season.

We still have a few weeks to go before seeds can actually be planted, but allow spring's freshness to fade. Why not try some new kinds of salad leaves from your local produce section? I recently had a salad of Belgian endive and fresh beets on a pilgrimage to Alice Water's legendary Chez Panisse, in Berkeley, CA. The endive sparked an awakening: instead of the traditional single leaf serving, which tastes like a wooden tongue depressor, I discovered that endive is delicious cut into disks. I came home feeling bold and inspired enough to create my own version of endive salad; I think you'll it love, too.

ENDIVE & RADICCHIO SALAD CHEZ DANNIES

Add to the salad bowl: 4–spears of endive, tough outer pieces removed, sliced into quarter inch disks; 1–head of radicchio, outer layer removed, sliced 'chiffonade' (into thin ribbons).

With clean hands, gently toss the lettuces with 3–T of Marie's Blue Cheese dressing. Plate the salad on four plates. Sprinkle 2–T of cooked and crumbled bacon among the four salads. Repeat with 2–T of crumbled blue cheese. Grind fresh pepper over the salads.

For homemade croutons, gently tear 2–slices of multigrain bread into rough cubes. Place in a quart sized plastic bag and toss in 1–T of olive oil and 1–t of granulated garlic (not garlic powder or garlic salt). Shake bag lightly to mix, pour croutons onto the baking sheet for a toaster oven. Toast croutons to medium color, just before serving. Divide equally. Serves 4.

EVERYDAY IS MOTHER'S DAY

MAY 4, 2006

Mother's day is May 14th, but it's not too early to start wondering (worrying) about it. Families wonder if they can possibly satisfy their very own wonder woman, and Mothers wonder if maybe this just might be the year that her clan will come through in storybook fashion: pressed pastel sheets on the bed, a beautiful Sunday morning breakfast tray set with fresh orange juice, strawberries in cream, cinnamon toast, hot free trade coffee and the New York Times hand delivered by Brad Pitt.

Dream on. After the soccer games, chores, chauffeuring, and general mayhem any spring Sunday brings, my family's momentum atrophies to a place where we end up eating the fabled Mother's Day meal off of a paper plate featuring spaghetti and Prego sauce, Jeff's 'specialty' (for which we are eternally grateful.)

But this year is going to be different! We've already had 'the talk' in anticipation of the holiday that never seems to happen. Jeff is going to grill something yummy and the girls are going to bake a cake. And I am going to stop reading magazines that read like fairy tales. And we're going to have a wonderful Mother's Day—right after we finish painting the house.

MOTHER'S DAY MOJITO CAKE

Preheat the oven to 325°F. Prep a Bundt pan by lightly coating the baking surface with soft butter and then dusting it with a small amount of flour. Tap out excess flour. Sprinkle 1–cup pecans or walnuts, onto the bottom of the pan.

To a prep bowl add 1–18 ounce yellow cake mix; 1–package Jell-O brand instant vanilla pudding; 4–eggs; ½–cup cold water; ½–cup vegetable oil; ½–cup dark rum.

Mix the cake ingredients together with an electric mixer, beating for 1 minute. Pour the batter over the nuts and bake for one hour. When the cake is baked, let it cool for 10 minutes; then, invert it onto a serving platter. Lightly score the top and spoon the glaze evenly over the top. Apply the glaze slowly, in small increments, for maximum saturation. Top with sections of fresh mint leaves.

Serves 8–10.

RUM GLAZE

In a small saucepan combine ¼–pound of butter; ¼–cup water; 1–cup granulated sugar; ¼–cup of fresh lime juice; 5–large mint leaves. Boil 3 minutes, stirring occasionally. Add ½–cup dark rum and boil 2 minutes longer. Remove mint leaves.

SCHWAG FOR THE GRILL MAN

JUNE 15, 2006

I recently attended a mountain bike clinic at Catamount presented by local pros Lea and Sabra Davison. These super-charged gals, Jericho natives and Middlebury alumni, are nationally sponsored by Trek and Devo. They taught us some smooth moves and gave us free Trek booty like water bottles and bike tools—but more importantly, they taught us some cool mountain biker slang.

The first word we learned was "chicked," as in a female rider who outmaneuvers or out performs a male rider. This instantly got me thinking about Father's Day and BBQing. Why? Well, let's face it: women are most likely to over-perform on 95% of the prep, execution, service, and clean-up of a typical BBQ. This includes planning the menu, purchasing food, prepping salads, and setting up plates, utensils and beverages. Also, they think ahead about marinades, timing, and any other necessary sauces, side dishes, and condiments. Big Daddy steps up to the grill with a beer and tongs and *Viola!*—he lays the meat on the grill. Expertly turning it (using one beer per side as a timing guide) and a hero-styled dinner is on the platter and headed for the table before you know it.

Ladies, here's where we want to be careful. Under no circumstances should you ever chick your mate on Father's Day. Resist the urge to monitor tongs, timing, or take any credit whatsoever for the food or festivities. Allow Dad to bask in the glory of a fabulous meal; let him do the victory lap as everyone cheers the world's greatest BBQer. That's what Father's Day is all about—making a great guy look good.

The second word we learned was schwag. This means prizes, free stuff and any other superfluous booty that makes a basic event extra special. In the case of Father's Day, grill schwag would be a fine idea for bolstering the grill performance. Every grill master requires a sauce mop and bucket; or, how about a set of 20" locking tongs with a flashlight built in? Wine barrel wood chips are sure to enhance flavor while double prong bamboo skewers are the latest in BBQ chic. I found these items and several more schwag-filled pages on Amazon.com.

For local last minute gifts truffle oil, Dijon mustard, balsamic vinegar, sea salt, premium olive oil, prime beef, and wet and dry rubs are all grill master essentials that would look great in a gift basket. How about a trip to the hardware store with the kids? Let them pick out a variety of paint brushes and a small pail to hold Daddy's new basting brushes.

Every grill master needs a pro to learn from. Stop by the bookstore and pick up any one of Steve Raichlen's six books on the art of BBQ. I'll bet my mountain bike he's never been chicked on this subject.

A LITTLE TASTE OF SUMMER

JUNE 29, 2006

Summer is officially here and Adam's Farm Market in Williston has proof positive: loads of native strawberries just waiting to find their way into ice cream, pie, jams, and my personal favorite, yummy summer coffee cakes. There is something old fashioned and comforting about a fresh fruit buckle. I like to get up early, pop one in the oven, and then take my dogs for walk while it bakes. I set my coffee maker on the automatic timer and return to the irresistible aromas of fresh cake and coffee. It smells so good my teenagers actually wake up earlier—just in time to share a little taste of summer before we scatter for the day.

SUMMER STRAWBERRY BUCKLE

Preheat oven to 350°F. Coat a Pyrex glass pie dish with cooking spray.

In a smaller prep bowl combine 2–cups white flour; 2–t baking powder; and ½–t salt. In a larger mixing bowl beat together 2–ounces soft butter; ¾–cup sugar; 1–egg; 1–t fresh orange zest; until fluffy.

To the butter add half of the flour mixture and ¼-c milk and lightly combine with a wooden spoon. Repeat with remaining flour and ¼–cup milk. Pour the stiff batter into prepared dish and move it around gently with a fork until evenly spread and lumpy looking.

Gently insert 2–cups hulled and chopped fresh strawberries into the batter using a chopstick. (Feel free to substitute raspberries or blueberries.) Cover the surface with streusel topping. Bake buckle for 55 minutes; serves 6–8.

STREUSEL TOPPING

Combine ½–cup chopped almonds; 2–ounces soft unsalted butter; ½–cup sugar; ⅓–cup flour; ½–t cinnamon with a fork until a crumbly mixture forms. Sprinkle over batter.

THE GOURMET CAMPER

JULY 13, 2006

Camping is a wonderful opportunity for sharing carefree time with friends and loved ones. Tenting on Burton Island, a hut–to-hut trek, or simply sleeping under the stars in the backyard—any kind of outdoor adventure has the power to create fond memories. Good grub is a big part of the pleasure. If you have matches and fuel then delicious, custom-crafted flatbreads are just a flicker away.

We freeze the flatbread dough coated with olive oil in a zip lock bag and use it to cool other pack items. It will thaw over 6 hours and then you can stretch it by hand. Place it directly on the rack of a gas or charcoal grill set at medium heat, or in a cast-iron pan or on a bed of triple thick foil for an open fire. Grill one side for 2–3 minutes, flip and then pile on the toppings: shredded cheeses, diced veggies, tomatoes, olives, artichokes, black beans and salsa, blueberry jam, butter and grilled mango. The stars are the limit. Cook 5–8 minutes more but watch it carefully—underdone is a little tastier than burnt. The breads are delicious hot or served cold for the next meal.

My husband, Jeff, and I still joke about a three-night backpack trip into New Hampshire's wild White Mountains twenty-five years ago. More of a pre-engagement litmus test, he was pretty happy to discover a cook, a tomboy, and a girlfriend wrapped into one package. The success of our trip hinged on good planning: dry gear, excellent meals, and the small bottle of Kahlua I stuck into the pack at the last minute. Each evening we'd sit in the cool river after dinner. Sweet sips of the coffee liqueur were scrupulously rationed for dessert. It taught us much about the wilderness called marriage: we learned how to how to share, how to budget, and–most importantly–how to savor… twenty-three years of marriage and still trekking!

CAMPER'S GRILLED FLATBREAD

Place 1–cup flour; and 1–cup semolina flour into a large bowl. Into a 2–cup measuring cup, add 1–cup of warm water; 1–package yeast; 1–t kosher salt; 1–T of honey salt; and 2–T olive oil. Stir lightly and let set for 5 minutes until frothy.

Add yeast mixture to flour and knead dough by gently incorporating ingredients. Add more flour or water if needed to form the dough to a soft ball. To freeze, divide dough and coat each ball with a film of olive oil. Place each ball in a quart sized Ziploc bag.

To use right away, let the dough rest in a clean, lightly oiled bowl for 1 hour or up to 8 hours, or covered overnight in the refrigerator. Recipe makes 2–10" flatbreads.

THE LEGEND OF SKIPPY

AUGUST 24, 2006

One lucky summer I lived on beautiful Martha's Vineyard for six months. I waitressed at a restaurant called 'The Ocean View' where the view was more of the liquor store than the ocean, but it had a quirky sort of character—just like the local folks I waited on and worked with. The most memorable of them was our prep cook, Skippy, a scarecrow of a man whose appetite for rum and slander would make Mel Gibson blush. I was terrified of Skippy at first—his idea of good fun was to scream like a banshee when our food orders were ready. But over time, I learned that behind Skippy's gruff façade lived a man with a heart as sweet as a ripe tomato who loved food passionately.

Skippy taught me to make Componata (com-po-na-da). It's like ratatouille but more distinctively Italian. Loaded with tomatoes, eggplant, onions, capers, and celery, it is the embodiment of summer's harvest. A simple bite of Componata can melt time and reunite me with my beloved Vineyard. That is the power of food.

Skippy showed me tricks, too, like what happens to a dish when vinegar and sugar come together with tomatoes to make magic. He taught me that fresh vegetables in August don't need much help to make them sing, and he introduced me to capers: pickled flower buds packed with a briny burst of flavor. But mostly, Skippy taught me that there are all kinds of beauty on an island—the views, to be sure, but also the kind of beauty that lives just below the surface of things.

MARTHA'S VINEYARD COMPONATA

Slice 4–stalks of celery into ¼-inch cuts; slice 3–medium onions into thin rings. Heat a large sauté pan with 2–T of olive oil and sauté the vegetables for 10 minutes. Add 3–finely chopped garlic cloves and sauté 1 minute more. Add 6–chopped Roma tomatoes, with seeds and juices, plus one 28–ounce can of crushed tomatoes.

Stir together ½–cup red wine vinegar and ¼–cup sugar. Slice 2–cups pitted black olives. Add olives, along with 4–T of capers and the vinegar mixture. Stir; cover and simmer for 10 minutes, then turn off heat.

Cut two medium eggplants into ½-inch cubes (skin remains on.) Heat a large sauté pan on medium high heat. Drizzle a little olive oil in the pan. Sauté the eggplant in batches until golden on all sides, drizzling in more olive oil as needed, up to ½–cup. (The eggplant will suck up the oil, so use sparingly.) Add eggplant to stockpot as you go. Combine mixture and let it set for a couple of hours. Serve hot or cold. Top with fresh basil and feta. Serves 10–12; freezes well.

EASING THROUGH THE SEASONS

SEPTEMBER 29, 2006

Soup season is upon us, so let us go gently into that good night by starting with a tomato based chowder that is served warm, not hot. You'll create a meal that is special enough for guests, but so easy it could become a family standard. Start by visiting the seafood section of your supermarket. See all those little cups filled with shucked clams, oysters, mussels, scallops, and shrimp? Buy a quarter pound of each or some small chunks of salmon, halibut and tuna—choose whatever combination you like, one to two pounds in all. Now, chop up some of those late season tomatoes, and you are on your way...

BLARNEY'S SEAFOOD CHOWDER

Heat a soup pot over medium heat; add 1–T of olive oil. Add 1–medium chopped sweet onion; sauté on low-heat for 10 minutes. Add 2–thinly sliced garlic cloves; sauté 2 minutes longer.

Deglaze pot with 1–cup white wine, scrapping up browned bits. Add 4–freshly chopped Roma or plum tomatoes, including seeds, skins and juice. Add a 28–ounce can of Redpack brand crushed tomatoes.

Add 1–cup of bottled clam juice and ½–cup orange juice. Simmer soup for 5 minutes; turn off heat. Add a few pinches of sea salt to taste. Add a pinch of red pepper flakes.

The soup can be made up to two days ahead at this point, store in fridge. To finish the soup, simmer for five minutes, turn off heat, then immediately add 1–2 pounds of your chosen seafood combination. Cover; set for five minutes. Stir and adjust seasonings to taste.

Roll 8 fresh basil leaves, cigar-style, and slice crosswise into a chiffonade (ribbons of basil). Serve soup in a shallow pasta bowl and top with basil, fresh pepper and a bit of freshly grated Parmesan cheese. Serves 6–8.

CHEESY BREAD

Heat oven to 375°F. Butterfly open 1–loaf of country-style bread. Place the loaves crust side down on a foil lined cookie sheet. Coat the bread with a thin layer of olive oil. Cut loaf across into quarters. Sprinkle loaves with one cup shredded mozzarella cheese. Pat gently to set. Bake in oven 10 minutes until bubbling and browned.

GOOD DEED HORS D'OEUVRES

OCTOBER 19, 2006

Last week I was in a cooking marathon. Friends were in charge of a cocktail reception for Champlain College's Single Parent Program and asked me to help select a menu and recipes. Once on board, I couldn't resist volunteering for the cooking part, too. Hors d'oeuvres are generally a weak spot for me (I think they are a lot of work) but I figured this event might serve as a canapé boot camp to jump-start me for the holidays. We cooked for days creating a thousand tasty bites that greatly pleased our guests. These are a couple of my favorite recipes; they are easy, gorgeous, and guaranteed to be welcomed at any party.

NIÇOISE CAKES

Spray an 18x13" bun pan (or cookie sheet with high sides) with non-stick spray. Preheat oven to 350°F. Heat a large pan and sauté 2–large chopped onions in 2–T of olive oil until caramelized, about 15 minutes. In a food processor chop 6–garlic cloves and 4–6 anchovies. Add 15–eggs, salt and pepper to taste, and process for 2 minutes. Pour mixture into the bun pan

Stir in 3–8 ounce cans of solid tuna in water, drained and flaked; 3–cups black olives, pitted; 3–cups of grape tomatoes, sliced; 3–cups mozzarella cheese; 1–cup fresh parsley or cilantro, chopped, scattering evenly.

This recipe can be prepped and refrigerated up to two days at this point. Bake for 35 minutes or until eggs look moist but firm.

When cool, cut into small squares; serve warm, or at room temperature. Makes 80–100 delicious bite sized pieces.

FONTINA AND ARUGULA FLATBREAD

Preheat oven to 425°F. Prep a large cookie sheet by sprinkling corn meal lightly over the surface.

Roll out 1–package of supermarket pizza dough into a long narrow rectangle that fits on the cookie sheet. Rub good quality olive oil lightly over the surface. Sprinkle 2–cups of shredded fontina cheese over the dough and bake for 11 minutes, or until bubbling and lightly browned.

Toss 3–handfuls of fresh arugula with 1–T of fresh lemon juice; gently press over the flatbread. Cut into serving sized squares. Grind fresh pepper lightly over the flatbread. 20 servings.

THE CUISINE OF CAIRO

NOVEMBER 16, 2006

The pungent air hangs like gauze soaked in cardamon, exhaust, and the sweat of 21 million people bustling for survival. The women, swaddled in layers of cloth, routinely court death as they sprint across wide streets filled with speeding bumper car rejects. At the crossroads of Africa and Asia, life teems with unvarnished riots of color and aromatic heat. Pyramids of saffron, sweet melon, and cabbage balance alongside ancient carts heaped with greens and bananas in a marketplace where butchers proudly carve fly-crusted meat for the masses. Children spot you and shout "Halloo!" and "Amerikans!" and with every step you feel freakishly foreign yet warmly welcomed. There is an exotic energy to the streets that is scary yet intoxicating. The poorest hawker will offer you a cup of tea or a coke if you happen to be shopping around 4:00 pm, the 'hour of hospitality.' Custom requires gracious acceptance, even to the offer of a cigarette, considered a special compliment. The call to prayer is a bewitching, mournful wail that permeates the city's loudspeakers five times daily as the devout hustle to pray. No matter where you go in Cairo there is always an arrow, even on the ceiling of a hotel room, pointing you towards Mecca. And the famous Nile flows like a powerful snake through the middle of this choreographed chaos, calmly protective of those who dwell in this compelling city.

Last week I visited my daughter, Kate, a student at the American University Cairo, along with my mom and a friend. Cairo had never been in the top ten of travel destinations for any of us, but when this opportunity arose we all jumped, albeit warily. Our friends thought we were crazy. We wondered: will we be safe? What will we do? And then, more enthusiastically, what will we eat?!

We felt completely safe and received a welcome sweeter than the honey soaked Kounafa we ate everyday of Ramadan. We stayed away from street food, eating in places that had treats like molasses with blue cheese and fresh figs on brown bread. Breakfast was often hearty leftovers, as well as eggs, yogurt and smoked fish.

Everyday we ordered mezze, an arrangement of bowls filled with fatoush (cucumber and tomato salad), tahini (ground sesame seeds and oil), hummus (chickpea mash), baba ganoush (eggplant puree), and olives, accompanied by fresh pita bread, often baked right in front of us. Artful nicoise salads, seafood pizza, calamari tempura, and poached fresh bass were favorite lunches. Grape leaves stuffed with rice and mint, shawarma (lamb or chicken on a rotisserie), beef kabobs, chicken curry, and cilantro studded jasmine rice were evening meals. Desserts were plentiful during the holiday of Ramadan: pistachio decked Baklava, rich date tarts, and Umm Ali (a hot raisin cake). Cairo is mysteriously exotic at first, but for those of us who favor a Mediterranean diet, well, *Bismillah!* (bon appetit). We were right at home in the global kitchen.

2007

CONFESSIONS OF A SELF-BASTER

JANUARY 4, 2007

Are you under-whelmed with odd kitchen gizmos masquerading as holiday gifts? You know what I'm talking about—pie weights that double as rosary beads, the celebrity set of a dozen melon ballers, or how about that bagel slicing kit? It's happened so often to me that my holiday nickname is now 'the self-baster.' I can't help it. I hate waste, don't horde, and revere form and function, so I often regift myself—immediately! I did this last Christmas and made one of my finest culinary purchases ever, a rice cooker. I returned a singing salad spinner and bought a National Brand SR MM10ns. I use it every week to cook perfect brown, basmati, wild, and Arborio rice.

With the New Year, a rice cooker has the potential to amaze and thrill your friends and family. The cooker is computerized to fit your schedule and menu demands. I am planning to whip up Saffron Vegetable Basmati Rice, plate it on a beautiful new platter (a gift I'm actually keeping), and fan grilled shrimp and beef kabobs around the edges. This entire meal will take thirty minutes to prep and serve, and it will feed 8–10 hungry people.

BASMATI BROWN RICE

This is our favorite because it is so fragrant and toothsome; supermarkets sell it in 3–pound jugs. Measure 3–cups of dry rice into the rice cooker; there is a measuring bar for water amounts inside the pot. To add intrigue and nutrition, toss in a few pinches of saffron (or any spice you like); a dash of olive oil; 2–pinches of kosher salt;

6–chopped garlic cloves; 2–handfuls of chopped onion; a handful of raw mushrooms; and 2–fistfuls of grape tomatoes. Then select from the cooking menu "brown rice" and hit the start button—it's that simple. You'll need to begin the cooking at least 3 hours before dinnertime for the rice to be ready, but you can begin cooking it up to 8 hours ahead. The rice will stay warm and make your kitchen smell amazing. Fluff with a chopstick and plate on a large platter for serving.

KABOBS

The kabobs are easy if you splurge on some premium shrimp and beef. Spear a few pieces on the short thick picks that are now available. Add some colorful sweet peppers. Sprinkle any combination of spice rub over the protein. Grill to desired doneness. Then fan around the platter of rice.

AIOLI SAUCE

How about a wow dipping sauce for the kabobs? In a small prep bowl stir together 2–cups of Hellmann's mayonnaise; 3–T of commercial chili garlic sauce; and 4–T of chopped fresh parsley or cilantro.

This is my ultimate self-baster meal: all of my favorite nutritious foods that yield maximum enjoyment and appreciation for the minimum amount of work. Form, function and no leftovers—sounds like a great way to begin 2007 to me.

BACK IN THE SADDLE

JANUARY 18, 2007

I had fun indulging over the holidays, did you? My favorite treat was a few sessions with a novel accompanied by mounds of chocolate almond bark and champagne. I think I got that suggestion from *French Women Don't Get Fat* by Mirelle Guiliano.

Supposedly, it takes twenty-one days to master a new habit. It's almost twenty-one days since I made the New Year's Diet Reform pledge and it's not going so well. Sure, I'm out there exercising, running with John Mayer crooning in my ipod ears: "..gravity, stay the hell away from me, keep me in the light.." has become my personal exercise mantra. (Surely not his artistic intention, but everything is relative.) The problem is that the exercise is simply not keeping up with gravity's evil twins, my saddlebags.

This is probably because my metabolism doesn't have a clue about which food season we are in. Why am I running in 40–degree weather and eating broiled scrod when this is supposed to be the dead of winter? Shouldn't we be slathering up the last dregs of beef stroganoff with tollhouse cookies or something? I feel more scrambled than the eggs for my chocolate soufflé.

Desperate for support and guidance, I decided to buy my first 'diet book'. I abhor the word diet, but this particular book *You: On A Diet: The Owner's Manual for Waist Management* by Drs. Mehmet Oz and Michael F. Roizen is something much more. With a funny, relaxed authority these heart surgeons explain that to change your body you have to know your body. In plain language they give you the skinny on body fat and physiology. They share what works ("Portions, People!"), blast diet myths, and dispense invaluable nutrition and recipe information.

Could over-consumption of food be part of a larger social problem? You bet it is if I can't fit into my dress jeans on a Saturday night. But seriously, it's a Social Problem on a grand scale. The USDA recently released disturbing numbers about hunger in America: 35 million people don't have enough food in our country, and 12 million of them are children. Vermont has a disproportionate share of these numbers. That's enough to kill anyone's appetite and hopefully trigger some awareness about our penchant for gigantic portions and mindless eating.

It got me thinking: can we support others as we strive to slim our waistlines? I'm making my waist management program a matter of mind over muffins by putting my money where the nacho chips used to flow. I figure that at least 10% of my weekly food bill is superfluous junk; by contributing that dollar amount towards healthy staples for a food shelf box I can do some good while bidding my saddlebags a permanent good-bye.

THE REST NEST

FEBRUARY 15, 2007

Jeff and I are now in the 'Rest Nest' phase of life—no children will be living in our home for twelve (glorious?) weeks. Quinn is in Costa Rica, Kate's in Cairo, and Tuckie is 3,000 miles away at UVM. It's a pleasant shock, softened by assurances that our flock will return in warm weather. As a result, I am having a bit of trouble recalibrating my kitchen to serve only two. Our midlife metabolisms are now slower than a crock-pot and my enthusiasm for mounting regular meals has wilted like week-old lettuce. I am not a happy cook.

Shopping is weird, too. I use a smaller cart and buy only a few things—milk lasts forever, and cereal, even longer. On my last shopping trip I caught myself fingering frozen entrees and took that as sure sign of food depression. Lynn, my favorite Hannaford cashier, wondered openly about the multiple cans of baked beans in my order.

It's ironic: I have more time than ever to indulge my hubby and entertain friends, but meals seem way more like a chore than they ever did before. For help in overcoming my culinary atrophy I asked my book club what they make for dinner now. They peppered me with fine suggestions: omelets and salad greens; splurges on prime fish; lamb chops; soups that last all week; and, my personal favorite, reservations.

The phone just rang and it's Miss UVM on the line, "Hi Mom, can I bring five of my friends home for dinner this Sunday night?" You know, I'm feeling pretty rested up. "Youbetcha, Sweetie."

QUICKIE PASTA FOR TWO (OR 4 OR 8…)

Boil water for pasta. In a large non-stick sauté pan heated with 1–t of olive oil, sauté one large sliced red onion along with 8–ounces of sliced mushrooms for 15 minutes, until caramelized. Add 3–pinches of kosher salt. In a small food processor finely chop 3–garlic cloves, the leaves of 2–rosemary stems, and the zest of a small orange.

To the onion mixture add ½–cup fruity red wine and 1–cup vegetable stock along with the garlic zest mixture. Cover and simmer on low while you boil a 9–ounce package of fresh fettuccini, about 5 minutes. Drain pasta and stir into the sauté pan along with ½–cup whipping cream. Combine, cover, and simmer on low for 2 minutes. Top with shredded Parmesan. Doubles or quadruples nicely.

BUILDING A BETTER MEAL

MARCH 1, 2007

Unless your child is some kind of food savant it's very doubtful that you'll ever find them rummaging around in the fridge shouting, "hey, where are those broccoli crowns?!" To encourage everyone in my family to eat more fruits and vegetables, especially during the cold winter months, I adopted a simple kitchen motto early on: 'Peel it and they will eat'.

I got started by setting up a daily grazing bar, a sure-fire way to get more of the food pyramid recommendations into daily consumption. I bought an attractive plastic rectangular tray and fitted six identical 2–cup glass bowls with tops to make a tapas-styled unit that looks great on my kitchen island. Everyday I fill the bowls with items like snap peas, baby carrots, grape tomatoes, celery sticks, cucumber coins, apple slices, pickles, sweet peppers, berries and peeled citrus fruits—you name it. It's amazing how fast the food goes when it is easily accessible. Kids and adults alike love it when they can spear food with a toothpick and dip. A tasty dip for both fruit and veggies is a cup of plain yogurt mixed with a ½–t of curry powder and 1–T of maple syrup, it's refreshing and delicious.

Exactly how much do we need in the way of fruits and vegetable everyday to maintain a healthy diet? MyPyramid is an updated version of the food pyramid that incorporates activity and moderation along with a proper mix of food groups. Quantities are now measured in cups and ounces instead of servings.

Visit mypyramid.gov and you'll find an excellent source of information. There are charts and detailed recommedations that are customized by the total calories an individual needs; lists of fruits and vegetables that make for a great shopping list; and there is a short video that explains the pyramid along with a special kid's section.

Another fun thing I did recently has earned me the name of 'gadget girl' but I don't care because I'm having too much fun with my Jack LaLanne Juicer that I picked up at Costco. Now I can juice raw beets, carrots, ginger, blueberries, and apples together in 30 seconds to make a divine elixir. One shot of this stuff sparks the cabin fever blues out of me in ten seconds flat, but usually I prefer to mix with it with seltzer and ice and sip on it all day long; it's the most delicious ginger-ale, without any sugar. The juicer comes with a great book of recipes and ideas for juicing and baking with the pulp. I find I never waste fruit or vegetables anymore as everything eventually gets juiced into something drinkable. Jack La Lanne is 92 and still going strong, proof that building a better meal will build a better me!

UMAMI IS THE FLAVOR MOMMY

APRIL 17, 2007

Japanese cuisine is among the most stunning and flavorful in the world. Asian chefs use the word umami (oou-mommy) to describe foods that are especially savory and delicious. It is thanks to the work of the Japanese scientist, Dr. Kikunae Ikeda, who first discovered that the amino acid glutamic was responsible for the umami taste in seaweed.

For centuries food tastes were categorized as either sweet, sour, salty, or bitter and it wasn't until 1908 that Dr. Ikeda identified the fifth flavor, umami. The glutamates common in protein-rich foods, ripe tomatoes, Parmesan cheese, cured ham, soy sauce, beef, oily fish, seaweed, and mushrooms are some of the curators of this earthy essence. The taste of umami itself is subtle, yet it blends well with other tastes expanding the flavors that make a dish more delicious.

Taste, smell, color, temperature, freshness, and appearance all combine to create the quality of a food's flavor. We immediately recognize the taste of sweet when we bite into a cookie or the sour pucker from a plump apple, but most palates don't immediately identify the quality of umami. Newborn babies naturally detest sour and bitter flavors and adore the sweet. But breastfed babies become instant experts on the wonders of umami and experience its magic every time they suckle their mother's breast milk, a protein source naturally rich in glutamates. (These babes are thinking "oou mommy, that's so good" and they don't care why.)

As cooks and eaters we already possess a natural instinct for aligning umami-rich ingredients. Traditional food pairings have endured for a reason—think tomato sauce sprinkled with Parmesan cheese, or grilled beef with mushrooms sautéed in butter. Next time you prepare a recipe, before you decide to pair down the ingredient list or substitute items, consider this: are you cheating your cuisine out of a layer of umami, and therefore extra flavor?

Umami has four roles in the kitchen to help cooks create more flavors on the plate. 1. Flavor Partner: add umami-rich mushrooms, or ham, and fortified wine to savory dishes. 2. Flavor Builder: use a tomato base, such as ketchup, and add soy, wasabi, fish sauce, brown sugar, or horseradish combinations to layer additional flavors. 3. Flavor Balancer: blend anchovies with mayo and raw garlic to soothe the bitter garlic and tame the unctuous mayonnaise. 4. Flavor Catalyst: in a roasted fish dish umami is the backbone flavor, yet it is nimble enough to welcome drops of lemon juice and pinches of salt to expand its primary flavor.

It may be known as 'the fifth flavor', but really, after exploring umami's epic influence on taste, I'm thinking that it is the mother of all flavors.

SOME LIKE IT HOT

APRIL 26, 2007

I ate my way around sunny Santa Fe, New Mexico, last week. A wonderland I have always wanted to visit, I was not disappointed. Dining choices are varied, superb, and reasonably priced. Santa Fe has the third largest fine art market in the US, exquisite galleries and museums abound. And here's the biggie: Santa Fe sponsors thirty-two miles of mountain bike single track within city limits! Needless to say, my palate, my eyes, and my quads were on overdrive the entire trip.

What's the seminal idea I learned about Southwestern cuisine? Hot stuff, baby—it's chipotle peppers. I found them in mayonnaise, salad dressings, omelets, polenta, margaritas, and even gingerbread. Chipotle (chee-POT-tleh) peppers are smoked jalapeno chili peppers. You'll most likely find them in powder form, or canned in adobo sauce, at the supermarket. Chipotle peppers are not for the faint of tongue. They pack a punch, and cooks must be careful to honor the 'less is more' mantra when employing them. Here's a great spring grilling idea to celebrate the Mexican holiday, Cinco De Mayo, which is right around the corner.

PORTABELLA BURGERS WITH CHIPOTLE MAYO

Combine ⅓–cup tequila and orange juice each, 2–T brown sugar, 1–t oil, 1–chopped chipotle pepper, and 2–crushed garlic cloves. Place 4–large portabella mushrooms in a gallon Ziploc bag and pour marinade over them. Marinate 1 hour. Meanwhile, sauté 2–large red onions, thinly sliced, in 1–T of olive oil until caramelized, about 15 minutes. Add ⅓–cup of sherry to deglaze; sauté 5 minutes more.

CHIPOTLE MAYONNAISE

Mince 1–chipotle chili (from a can packed in adobo sauce) into a paste to make a heaping teaspoon. Combine it with 1–cup of mayonnaise and a pinch of kosher salt. Add ¼–t of adobo sauce and mix well. Adjust for your own heat tolerance; this recipe is medium hot.

Grill the portabella mushrooms on a hot grill for about 5 minutes per side, depending upon their thickness. They should be soft but not soggy. Layer them whole on a light bakery-style bun or brioche, or slice the mushrooms steak style and layer on a toasted whole wheat English muffin. Top with red onions, shredded iceberg lettuce and lots of mayo. Serves 4.

AN HOUR OF LOVE

MAY 10, 2007

The word enthusiasm means "filled with God." The Greeks must have had mothers in mind when they coined this term. Who else on the planet gets more excited about potty seats, ant farms, or mediocre test scores than a mom? Why not share a little enthusiasm with a beloved mom this weekend by cooking up a nice dinner: most of the moms I know would rather watch family members enjoying an hour in the kitchen together than wait an hour in line for dinner out. This fun menu is easy cooking for all ages. And, it's OK if mom just happens to pick up the main ingredients on her weekly shopping trip, we can't expect her to shut down the Goddess completely!

JOB 1: GINGER SPLASH

Settle mom down comfortably with the weekend papers and a make her a treat: combine 2–shots of tequila or rum (optional) with crushed ice, a small piece of crushed fresh ginger, and a tablespoon of chopped mint all topped off with Reed's Ginger Beer.

JOB 2: BLUEBERRY CORNBREAD

Follow directions on a standard box of cornmeal, but use buttermilk instead of milk. Add 1–cup of fresh blueberries to the final batter and bake for 25 minutes at 350ºF. Serve with soft butter.

JOB 3: BBQ CHICKEN

Quarter several Cornish game hens or small chickens (plan on 2–pieces/person). Place in a gallon Ziploc bag and douse with Ken's Lite Caesar Dressing. Set aside for 30 minutes then grill chicken about 20–25 minutes on medium heat. Wrap in heavy foil and let rest.

JOB 4: BBQ SAUCE

Pour a commercial bottle of BBQ sauce into a small saucepan. Embellish the sauce with 1–t of powdered ginger; ¼–cup of orange juice; ¼–cup soy sauce; and a shot of Tabasco sauce. Stir well and simmer 10 minutes until thick. Adjust seasoning to taste.

JOB 5: ASPARAGUS

Snap the ends off of fresh asparagus and toss lightly in 1–T of olive oil. Grill lightly turning evenly for 5 minutes on low heat grill. Place on a serving dish and sprinkle with kosher salt, a splash juice from an orange, and some chopped fresh mint on top. Serve at room temperature.

JOB 6: CAESAR SALAD

In a small processor add the zest of half a lemon; and 2–garlic cloves; mince well. Add 2–T of fresh lemon juice; 1–cup Hellman's mayonnaise; a pinch of salt; and 2–t of anchovy paste (optional). Blend well. Chop heads of pre-washed romaine lettuce (1 head/2 people) and place in a large bowl. Just before serving, toss in half the dressing and sprinkle with shredded Parmesan cheese and freshly ground pepper. Add dressing if needed.

JOB 7: ICE CREAM

Scoop out bowls of the family favorite, or take mom out for a cone.

ANTI-HERO

MAY 24, 2007

For some women, cowboys are their weakness; for me it's bacon, bleu cheese, and French fries. To counter my dereliction, I try to eat these foods with salad greens, an excellent antioxidant-rich foil. Why do we need antioxidants in our diet? Because they are the good guys roaming the range after the outlaws (free radicals.) Sure, some free radicals appear normally during metabolism and aid in immune function, but mainly they contribute to neurodegenerative disease, chronic inflammatory disease, cancer, cardiovascular disease and aging.

Environmental factors such as campfire and cigarette smoke, radiation, and herbicides are also members of the free radical gang. The antioxidant's job is to hunt these bad boys down, arrest them, and then lock 'em up before they can do any more harm. You are a hero to your body every time you choose antioxidant-rich foods.

Normally the body's sheriff can handle free radicals just fine, but when things get rowdy (if antioxidants are unavailable or the free-radical production becomes excessive) damage to organs and skin occurs. Because this process accumulates with age, NOW is the perfect time to join the super salad posse by adding fresh summer greens, herbs and spices to the mix. Consider growing produce in outdoor containers filled with herbs and lettuces for optimal nutrition

Herbs such as sage, rosemary, oregano, and thyme are antioxidant-rich. Marjoram leaves yield a double dose of the age repelling good stuff. Vegetables such as artichokes, beetroot, broccoli, garlic, leeks, radish, onions and spinach add extra cell-protecting phenols. To boost nutrition from bowl to belly play with combinations that include pinto beans, blueberries, cranberries, pecans, walnuts, and hazelnuts. Dressing presents another opportunity to increase the antioxidant quotient of the super salad. Extra-virgin olive oil is a must combined with healthful sherry or wine vinegars. Lemon flavored flax seed oil is my new favorite oil for salad dressings with a dash of Dijon mustard and champagne vinegar. Cumin, cinnamon, clove, garlic, honey, maple syrup and fresh ginger are also excellent sources of flavor and antioxidants for dressing condiments.

Whip dressings up in small quantities with 1:2 ratio of vinegar to oil to create the base; add additional condiments in small quantities, adjusting for flavor as you emulsify.

Nobody wants to end up looking like the Marlboro man, so douse the butts, slap on the sunscreen, and giddy-up to the salad bowl for a youthful, healthy summer!

HOT DOG DAYS

AUGUST 17, 2007

It's hot and sultry—the dog days of summer—and the only foods I really want to eat require no utensils. That means hot dogs, pork ribs, chicken legs, corn on the cob, and watermelon.

Why do we call this period 'the dog days'? Eons ago, when the night sky was free of artificial light and smog, people visualized shapes in the sky by connecting the dots of stars. Canis Major (the big dog) is Sirius, the brightest star in the night sky. During late July Sirius is aligned with the sun. It was so bright that people believed the earth received heat from it, creating a stretch of hot and sultry weather. They named this period of time, twenty days before the conjunction to twenty days after, 'the dog days' after Sirius.

Doggonit, I think the best way to weather this weather is to whip up a batch of my Mom's amazing BBQ sauce, slather it all over hot dogs, ribs, and chicken—and eat with my hands!

PAT MYETTE'S FAMOUS BBQ SAUCE

In a large saucepan sauté ¼–cup celery, finely diced; ½–cup green bell pepper, finely diced; and ½–cup onion, finely diced; in 2–T olive oil for 5 minutes.

Add 3–12 ounce bottles chili sauce; 1–cup ketchup; ½–cup brown sugar (firmly packed); 3–T VT maple syrup; ¼–cup cider vinegar; 1–clove garlic; 2–T dry mustard; 2–T seasoning salt; 2–T Worcestershire sauce; 1–T chili powder; 2 or 3–t Liquid Smoke; 1–t white pepper; 1–t cumin; 1–t black pepper; ½–t red pepper flakes; ½–t gumbo file powder. Simmer gently over low heat, covered, for 1 hour.

Cool sauce then store in clean glass jars in the fridge; lasts several weeks. Recipe makes about 4–12 ounce jars.

(Pat's Testing Note: "This sauce comes out different EVERY time I make it—measurements are not precise!")

A FEW OF MY FAVORITE (NEW) THINGS

SEPTEMBER 27, 2007

During summer travels I discovered some fun new food ideas to share with hungry readers. We traveled to the Pacific Northwest to deliver Quinn to college in Portland, Oregon, and found ourselves in a foodie Mecca! These folks are particularly serious about tea, wine, and chocolate. Portland is a funky town filled with more than a dozen artisanal chocolate shops—fig and fennel truffles, anyone?

Forty-five minutes west of Portland is Dundee, smack in the heart of the Willamette Valley wine country. Over 100 area wineries produce pinot noir. We fell in love with the rich berry-chocolate pinots produced by Archery Summit (available in Vermont). We visited our favorite winemaker, Argyle, sampling their $25 Brut, which is the best sparkling wine available for the price point. The wine was fine, but our stay at The Black Walnut Inn was the highlight, accented by an incredible breakfast of Green Eggs & Ham. Organic eggs were tossed with a thin spinach puree and scrambled. They were served atop a soft brioche toast laden with slices of Canadian ham.

After breakfast, we had a nice Dr. Seuss day traveling to Cannon Beach, a savvy destination for surfing. We worked up quite an appetite on the boards as we frolicked and dumped in the frigid water and sunshine. The Chef/Owner of The Nehalem Inn amazed us with simple yet exquisitely prepared local food. Try plating several quartered heirloom tomatoes of various colors on a platter of fresh arugula. Lightly drizzle on lemon vinaigrette, adding small pinches of sea salt. Top with crumbled Point

Reyes Blue Cheese (available at Fresh Market) and fresh pepper. This salad is so gorgeous and delicious that we ate it three nights in a row. Coleslaw had very thin strips of ripe mango and a rice vinegar and sesame oil dressing. The fruit made this standard jump for joy with flavor. We ate lots of oysters, too. The fried oysters were especially scrumptious and we learned that the secret to a good batter is evaporated milk with a flour/cornmeal combination.

Our afternoon refresher was simply iced coffee. But when it is made with fresh espresso, cream, and simple syrup—well, we got very selective, very quickly, about this afternoon treat. To replicate, I now just save a cup from my morning brew, but the simple syrup is essential: measure 4–cups of sugar into an easy-pour container. Add ½–cup of boiling water and stir with a chop sick. Add additional ½–cup boiling water, cap, shake well, and store in fridge.

Need a little something to go with that coffee? Warm up a pan. Spread Nutella and soft goat cheese on the flip side of two buttered slices of baguette to make a grilled cheese sandwich that will blow your mind. I could go on–and I will–in my next column. Give these goodies a try for now!

SLEEPLESS IN SEATTLE

OCTOBER 11, 2007

Did you ever eat so much you couldn't sleep? The second part of our Pacific Northwest tour was a fiftieth birthday visit to Seattle and my best pal from high school, Cindy Smullen Blais. Cindy staged a bacchanalia that Ratatouille and his extended family could have feasted on happily for weeks. Seattleites are very serious about their food—and, no surprise, it is sensational stuff. The fresh fish choices alone made me wonder aloud about relocating, not to mention the unique array of heirloom vegetables, flowers, herbs, and hazelnuts available at the corner market. I'd never even heard of white salmon before this trip. It is a thick, rich, meaty salmon that we roasted with lemon and buttered garlic croutons—incredible! All weekend we ate, reminisced, ate, laughed, stayed up late, and ate some more.

Cindy really rolled out the red tablecloth, stuffing us with fresh chocolate chip cookies and brownies for a bike tour along the boardwalk. Then she popped us into the hot tub overlooking Seattle's Space Needle skyline with gin & tonics.

Next, she whipped out delicate puff pastry pinwheels filled with prosciutto & Parmesan and served them with a perfectly chilled local Chateau Ste. Michelle Ethos. The grilled lemongrass beef and dill scented rice for dinner each had little complements that married beautifully with a Leonetti Cellars, 2002 Reserve Cabernet from Walla Walla. (I won't even mention the white chocolate cheesecake with candles.)

Thanks to Chef Cindy, I had a fabulous 50th as we ate, reminisced, ate, laughed—and then cried when we parted. As soon as we boarded the plane I paged Dr. Nod and slept all the way to Vermont.

CINDY'S YUMMY EGG & SAUSAGE CASSEROLE

Brown and crumble 1 ½–pounds of breakfast sausage in a sauté pan. Remove the crusts on 9–slices of white sandwich bread and cube the bread. In a prep bowl beat together 9–eggs; 1–t kosher salt; 1–t dry mustard; 2 ½–cups of shredded cheddar cheese; 3–cups of 2% milk. Add sausage and bread. Pour into a greased 9x13" pan. Cover and refrigerate for at least 12 hours. Bake in a preheated 350°F oven for 1 hour prior to serving. Slices reheat beautifully in the microwave. Serves 10–12.

50 WAYS TO LEAVE YOUR BLUBBER

NOVEMBER 22, 2007

If you spent Thanksgiving on the Pepto Bismol channel, maybe it's time for a little review of healthy eating strategies as we enter the time of year I refer to fondly as "the nexus of eating nirvana" (aka the holiday season.) The goal here is to enjoy traditional foods–especially nostalgic treats–and still welcome 2008 with open arms that don't threaten the physical safety of children and small animals. Have your jeans passed their expiration date? The answer is 'Yes' if your legs could possibly be mistaken for sausage casings, or, if muffin tops are blowing out your belt loops. Here are some hot health tips for a svelte segue into 2008:

1. Drink lots of water. 2. Skip simple carbohydrates that spike blood sugar. 3. Exercise everyday that you plan to eat. 4. Choose soy products to raise healthy HDL. 5. Prep healthy meals and snacks ahead. 6. Run or walk 3 miles 3–4 times a week. 7. Keep a food diary. 8. Lower cortisol levels with meditation. 9. Stubb the butts. 10. Take a dance class. 11. Switch to whole-wheat pastas. 12. Mix cider, pomegranate, or blueberry juice with seltzer for antioxidant rich cocktails 13. Walk everywhere possible. 14. Sip green tea—it's a fat burner. 15. Detox at Bikram hot yoga. 16. Put wilted organic spinach into everything savory. 17. Sauté foods. 18. Avoid fried foods. 19. Get a deep tissue Thai massage. 20. Eat half sized portions of meals. 21. Consume whole foods and grains. 22. Get an acupuncture tune-up. 23. Eat lots of fiber, garlic, and onions. 24. Sleep more. 25. Substitute organic baby purees for fat. 26. Cardio: go slow, go long. 27. Weigh your food. 28. Do 2 shorter workouts a day. 29.

Hire a personal trainer. 30. Workout to music you love. 31. Steam, don't boil, food. 32. Listen to *French Women Don't Get Fat* audio book. 33. Join a gym. 34. Find a dog to walk. 35. Lift weights 3x weekly. 36. Get a thorough check-up. 37. Write down specific fitness goals. 38. Stay motivated with cross training. 39. Keep fueled with healthy snacks. 40. Supplement with vitamins. 41. Spice up recipes with exotic mixtures from Penzeys.com. 42. Wine is fine, but 8–ounces is tops. 43. Make sure training shoes fit well. 44. Go to PT to remedy pain and prevent injury. 45. Use % body fat and tape measurements, not actual weight, to monitor success. 46. Taste everything, but train your brain and eyes about portion size. 47. Find a fitness partner. 48. Try something new each week—a class, conditioning exercise, or route. 49. Enjoy a little dark chocolate everyday. 50. Enjoy yourself and cherish your body.

We've all heard these suggestions before, but there has never been a better time to incorporate a few new strategies into a health game plan. On New Year's Eve, when that ball drops to welcome in 2008, you'll be looking and feeling fantastic. Bye-bye blubber!

A CONVENIENT PROOF

DECEMBER 6, 2007

W. C. Fields said "I always cook with wine, sometimes I even add it to the food."

Alcohol is a valuable ingredient in cooking because at low concentrations it trips the release of fruity esters and aroma molecules into the air. As alcohol dissipates during cooking, the unique quality of the spirit or wine lingers, creating enhanced flavor and complexity to a dish. I know this is true—my Margaritaville Marinade without tequila is simply wasted, and a Harvey Wallbanger Cake without Galliano? No thanks.

When I make tomato soup I start with 3–28 ounce cans of crushed tomatoes. I always add 3–ounces each of vodka and orange juice along with vegetable stock. The orange juice cuts any tin flavor and the vodka rockets the tomatoes. When vodka is added to tomatoes it stimulates the release of flavor molecules that water or fats cannot. In cooking, alcohol is kind of gender confused and acts a little like fat and a little like water. Also, vodka doesn't have any flavor of its own to impart, so the result is an intensely concentrated tomato flavor. Toss in some caramelized onions deglazed with a bit of sherry and freshly chopped garlic, season and simmer for 30 minutes (the alcohol burns off), and you've got yourself one hummer of a soup.

OK, so have some fun with this, but remember—chef's rule of tongue: one drink while cooking is beautiful, two gets ugly. No lamp shades for toques in the kitchen. Here's a festive holiday dish to get you started.

DRUNKEN DATE STUFFED PORK TENDERLOIN

Butterfly 2–pork tenderloins, slicing the length of the pork, three quarters of the way deep. Place plastic wrap over the pork and pound lightly until it lies flat.

In a glass bowl place 1–cup of pitted dates, rough chop. Cover with 4–ounces of sherry (not cooking sherry—get your stuff from the liquor store.) Cover with plastic and micro on HI for 1–2 minutes. Let steep as dates plump up absorbing the sherry

In a food processor, pulse together 4–garlic cloves and the zest of an orange. Pulse in 1–cup shredded Gyuere cheese, 1–cup fresh cranberries, 1–T each of fresh rosemary and thyme leaves.

Gently mix processed ingredients in with the dates. Mix in 1–cup shelled pistachios and ½–t of powdered clove. Pack mixture evenly onto the 2 flat tenderloins. Season with salt and pepper. Roll up like a jellyroll and tie with butcher string in several spots. Place seam side down in a roasting pan and rub all over with olive oil. Roast at 400°F for 35–40 minutes. Remove from oven and tent with foil; rest for 20 minutes. Slice and serve on a bed of wild rice. Serves 6.

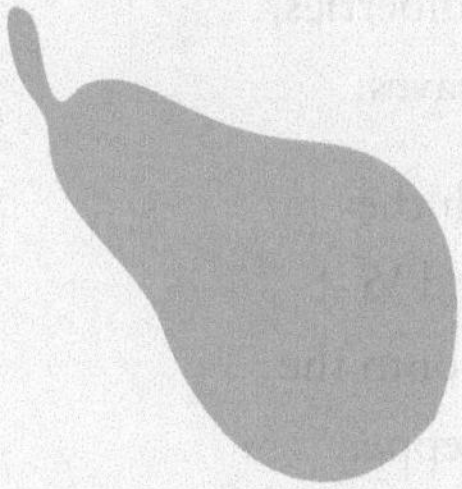

2008

ROMANCING THE KITCHEN

FEBRUARY 7, 2008

We've all heard the axiom that the way to a man's heart is through his stomach. But did you know that the way to a woman's heart is through her ear? If you really want to get your honey's heart a hoppin' this Valentine's Day all you have to do is nuzzle in and say, "Darling, why don't I make us a special dinner tonight?" Call me crazed by Cupid's arrow, but there is nothing sexier than a man cooking in the kitchen—all that focus, passion, and love pouring into the food. It's a beautiful thing. You'll win your Valentine's heart by preparing this simple but special Bolognese Sauce (say "bo-lo-naze"). As the pots clang and your love's ears buzz, prep some garlic bread. When you begin to whip up the chocolate hazelnut apricots please remain alert—your date may flat out faint from astonishment. Even if you don't happen to find yourself particularly in love on this holiday, be the cupid of your own kitchen and treat yourself to a delicious meal.

JEFF'S BOLOGNESE SAUCE

In a large skillet heat 1–T of olive oil. Add I–cup chopped onion and 1–cup diced carrot; sauté for 15 minutes. Add 4–chopped garlic cloves, sauté for 2 minutes more. Deglaze pan with a mixture of 3–ounces each of vodka, orange juice, and water. Add a 25.5–ounce jar of Muir Glen organic fire roasted tomato pasta sauce. Add large pinches of dried basil and oregano. Season sauce with pinches of kosher salt, and a small pinch of red pepper flakes. Cover and simmer on very low for 20 minutes.

Meanwhile, bring a large pot of lightly salted water to a boil. Heat another skillet and fry 1–pound of lean hamburger, breaking up the meat into small chunks. Drain the excess fat and add meat to the sauce. Boil 1–pound of dried pasta for 10 minutes; drain. To finish the sauce, taste for seasoning and then lightly stir in 2–T of mascarpone cheese. Portion out pasta into bowls, top with sauce, and sprinkle freshly grated Parmesan cheese on top. Serves 2 for dinner and 2 for breakfast.

CHOCOLATE HAZELNUT APRICOTS

Toast a handful of hazelnuts or almonds in the toaster oven for 2 minutes. Cool and seal in a plastic sandwich bag. Crush the nuts. In a glass bowl combine 2–t of vegetable oil and 6–ounces of best quality dark chocolate chips; microwave until just melted, 2 minutes. Choose 8–10 nicely shaped dried apricots. Dip half of the fruit section into the chocolate, and then dip chocolate part into the nuts. Place on a cookie sheet lined with parchment. Wedge a few festive pieces of fruit into scoops of vanilla ice cream garnished with a fresh mint sprig.

WAITING FOR GOOD DOUGH

FEBRUARY 21, 2008

The February Creep is upon us. It's that doughboy bulge on the belly caused by our efforts to battle winter weather with the likes of Shepard's Pie and Double Decadence Fudge Brownies. In my efforts to combat The Creep I'm trying to eat hearty foods, but choosing the ones with a lower glycemic index. Low GI foods are whole foods with little sugar content and lots of fiber and roughage. For a healthy bread source, I've been baking my MultiGrain Rolls. These are easy to make, despite the time it takes for two dough rises. I use a quick rise yeast to move things along faster. MulitGrain rolls are definitely worth the wait, and everybody will enjoy them—especially if it is 'good for you' dough.

MULITGRAIN ROLLS

Fill a 1–cup glass measuring cup with 4–ounces of warm water. Add ¼–ounce of quick rise yeast (1 packet). Add 3–ounces of maple syrup. Stir and let sit a few minutes until foamy. Boil some water and add 8 ounces to ⅓–cup of bulgur. Let the bulgur sit until water is absorbed.

Place the dough hook in a food processor and measure in 3–cups of King Arthur's white whole wheat flour; 1–cup white flour; 4–ounces of corn meal; 1–cup rolled oats; 3–T sesame seeds; 3–pinches of kosher salt and blend well.

With the motor running add the proofed yeast and another cup of warm water. Process the dough until it is gently pulling off the sides of the work bowl. If it is too dry, add small amounts of warm water to get things moving. Too wet? Add small amounts of flour.

Roll dough onto a floured work surface and knead lightly until it forms a nice compact disk. Lightly oil a large glass bowl and place dough in the bowl.

Cover lightly with a clean cloth and let it rise for 30 minutes. When you can poke two fingers into the dough and an imprint remains, place dough on a floured work surface and knead lightly.

Break up the dough into small balls and form rolls that are about 2" across. Place them on parchment covered baking sheets far enough apart so they have room to double in size. Cover with a clean cloth.

Heat the oven to 375ºF. Let the rolls rise for 30 minutes and then brush each roll with an egg white glaze (dilute 1–egg white with a little water.) Sprinkle some extra oats and sesame seeds on the top of the glazed rolls and bake for 20 minutes. Makes 16 rolls.

THE ORGANIC PANIC

MAY 5, 2008

Unless you've been living under a pile of compost, you've been exposed to green-media and the campaign for eating mainly organic and local foods. The locavore trend is about eating more products produced closer to home and it's a topic dearer to magazine editor's healthy hearts than saturated fat. (Locavore was even 'the 2007 word of the year' for the American Oxford Dictionary). The organic movement, once a label is now a full-blown lifestyle. And it's a bit more complicated what with actual standards manipulated by elected officials and all. Did you know that Walmart is going organic? This is not a good thing. Walmart—notorious for keeping costs down–is lobbying hard with deep pockets to compromise certification standards that are fragile, at best. The pressure will force the collapse of small, local producers who we currently support. It's like discovering your evil twin weeding the vegetable patch with a weed whacker.

Personally, I love organic products and living green; after all, Vermont is the Green Mountain State. Yet, when I try to fill my shopping cart with certified organic, free–trade, produced in Vermont labels, my once healthy heart starts to beat unnaturally fast, and a peculiar ringing starts in my ears, and suddenly, I am having a full blown price tag panic attack among the biodynamic Vidalia onions. What's a conscientious eater to do? I mean, a local 8–ounce rib-eye steak for $26.95? Organic line-caught wild Seattle salmon at $15.98 a pound? 8–ounces of Organic Valley bacon at $8.19 shipped from California? Wouldn't I be better off choosing Vermont Smoke House bacon for less than 5 bucks, even if it is not organic? We are in the middle of an organic-locavore smack down.

Eggs and dairy products? I can absolutely taste the difference in quality. And I buy organic-local products only (though I must admit, I didn't start doing this until my girls moved out.). Produce? Organic produce contains 27% more vitamin C, 21% more iron, and 29% more magnesium than traditionally grown foods. Surely organic tomatoes, lettuces, and fruits taste better, but I'm not convinced that organic avocados, frozen sweet peas, and dish detergent are essential items in my cart. Doing the right thing for the local economy, for a healthy lifestyle, and for the environment. Common sense tells me that a Macintosh apple from Williston is a better choice than organic Fujis from New Zealand.

With soaring food prices, sourcing summer produce from a local CSA (Community Supported Agriculture) or local farmer's market, is the most cost-effective and healthy way to eat, short of growing your own. This would be an excellent use of your stimulus check; talk about supporting the locavore movement! Bottom line: don't panic or grow manic over the subject of organic; awareness is about healthy choices, and stressing about food is wasted time. Simply choose the best that is available to you at the moment. If the organic produce happens to look a little beat, it's fine to grab something fresher, give it a good rinse, and enjoy it. Eating fruits and vegetables is always good for your diet, and a little local bacon won't hurt either.

SISTER-HOOD OF THE TRAVELING PALATES

JULY 10, 2008

In my next life, I want to come back as one of my daughters. Kate's in Cairo, in love; Tuckie is Euro-backpacking; and Quinn is tracking turtles in Greece. My friends want to know how I sleep at night. All I need to know is: #1. Are the sisters are safe? #2. What they are eating? By collecting food tidbits I can intuit how far into the culture they are delving, and generally gauge how the trips are going. My finicky eater, Christine, has grown by leaps and bounds emailing me detailed reports of encounters with delicious classics. So, just in time for local tomatoes, let's take our own flavor trip together!

CATALONIAN SHRIMP (BARCELONA, SPAIN)

In a hot cast iron pan on high heat, add 1–T of olive oil. Add 1–cup chopped fresh tomatoes, including seeds and juices and sprinkle with kosher salt. Stir and add 2–large garlic cloves, finely sliced; and 10 extra–large shrimp, peeled and deveined. Cook for 2–3 minutes stirring constantly until the shrimp turn bright pink. Add a dash of white wine to keep the tomatoes from drying out.

Toast 4–slices of artisanal sourdough bread. Finish the shrimp by stirring in 1–T butter and 2–t best quality balsamic vinegar. Place the toast on plates and portions of the shrimp and sauce onto the slices. Top with sea salt and fresh pepper and a toss of basil ribbons. Serves 2 for a meal, or 4 for a starter.

CAPRESE SALAD (CAPRI, ITALY)

You'll need: fresh mozzarella cheese; fresh tomato slices; fresh arugula leaves; fresh basil leaves; 4-ounces of a spicy deli ham, cut into small cubes; best quality olive oil; sea salt and fresh pepper.

On each salad plate place a small handful of lightly torn arugula and basil leaves. Slice two pieces of fresh mozzarella cheese and one tomato per serving plate. Sprinkle a bit of ham onto each salad. Lightly swirl olive oil over the salads and add pinches of salt and a sprinkle of pepper. Allow salads to sit at room temperature for 1–2 hours. Serve with good bread and a crisp Pinot Gris.

SHUCKING UP TO CORN

JULY 24, 2008

With food prices spiking it's more important than ever to choose peak nutritious produce that doesn't allow for waste. Last week I paid $6.79 for a dozen ears of corn at a farm stand in the Northeast Kingdom. In my checkbook that makes corn a freshly minted luxury. Egregiously overpriced? I thought so. Wasteful? Not on my watch.

After peeling the ears–and taking a bit more time to coo, relish, and fawn over the noble stalks–I coated the VIPs (very important produce) lightly in canola oil and grilled them on a hot gas grill. This is the best way to cook corn on the cob, turning each ear until lightly browned as the corn sugar begins to caramelize. This takes only a few minutes. Next, I wrapped the ears lovingly in the cook's equivalent of the Green Room (heavy-duty aluminum foil) to rest until mealtime.

Leftovers yielded two ears, so I gently shucked the cobs; I also scavenged all other knobs of cobs where eaters had done a poor job, letting nary a precious kernel go astray. I ended up with 4–cups of corn. I put all of the cobs in a large pot of cold water and simmered them for 20 minutes creating a nice starchy vegetable broth for future corn chowder that would feature 3–cups of the jewels.

In constant pursuit of transforming the plain into the sublime, the fourth cup of corn is where I really hit my stride. I combined some cooked orzo with the corn and a few other savories to make one of the easiest and most delicious risotto-style dishes ever. I used mascarpone, which I recommend not only for it's truly epic flavor, but also for the consistency it delivers to the dish and the fact that a very small amount makes for an incredibly creamy, dreamy forkful. I think of mascarpone like an expensive perfume—a small amount goes so far, and there really is no substitute for the finest of products.

So, this summer let the humble kernel rule. Give our newly precocious, always precious, corn the unstinting adulation and devotion it deserves.

ORZCORPONE

Boil 1–cup of orzo pasta, according to the package directions. Drain and rinse in cold water. Finely slice 2–garlic cloves and 1–shallot. In a sauté pan melt 1–T of butter over medium heat and add the garlic and shallot. Sauté for 5 minutes, but do not allow the ingredients to color. Add 1–cup of reserved corn, the orzo, and ⅓–cup of vegetable stock. Let it simmer 5 minutes, stirring gently. Stir in 1–T of mascarpone (heaping.) Taste, then season with kosher salt and fresh pepper. Serve with a sprinkle of fresh Parmesan cheese and a chiffonade of fresh basil. Serves 2–4.

GRAZIN' IN THE GRASS

AUGUST 21, 2008

I had a Vermont 'staycation' last week and it was a blast. I visited Shelburne Farms for the Vermont Fresh Network event; learned about primal cuts at a workshop on grass-fed meats; saw the Mary Cassatt exhibit at the Shelburne Museum; biked up ApGap; and ate a maple cremee from the Sunoco station everyday. At the Richmond farmer's market I splurged on grass-fed porterhouse steak from Maple Wind Farm in Huntington (maplewindfarm.com) that was so good it made my eyes roll back in my head. The meat is lean and juicy and herbal tasting. It requires less time on the grill and a 20–minute resting period in foil. I gave it a slather of Laudemio olive oil and a big pinch of sea salt. Paired with a Columbia Valley pinot noir, Helix 2004, (spied at Fresh Market on Pine Street) it was simple perfection. For side dishes I lightly mashed some baby potatoes called "cranberry" that are bright purple inside. They looked stunning with snipped chives and a glistening knob of butter. A lightly steamed rainbow of fresh green, yellow, and purple beans made for a quick salad. Who needs an airport? In the summer, among Vermont's gorgeous green pastures, vacation simply doesn't get any better than this.

FARMER'S MARKET SALAD

Trim 2–pounds of mixed fresh garden beans into thirds. Rinse. Place in a glass bowl with a film of plastic wrap. Zap in micro for 2 minutes. Remove wrap, pour beans into a colander, and sprinkle with kosher salt and pepper. Place 2–bunches of fresh baby greens on a serving plate. Add beans and top with 8–cherry tomatoes; sliced in half; ¼–cup toasted pine nuts; and 4–ounces Vermont goat cheese; crumbled. If you have any stray fresh herbs, toss those in, too. Using a zigzag motion pour desired amount of dressing over the salad. Serves 4.

SUNNY MAPLE MUSTARD DRESSING

The turmeric is what gives this dressing a sunny color. If you don't have any, don't sweat it, but it is a fun spice to play with in small amounts.

In a small food processor chop 2–garlic cloves. Add a pinch of turmeric, ⅓–cup fresh lemon juice; 1–T of Dijon mustard; 1–T of maple syrup; and a large pinch of kosher salt. Blend for 30 seconds. With motor running add ⅓–cup of olive oil in a stream; blend about 2 minutes, until the mixture emulsifies slightly. Yields ¾–cup.

FARMER BROWN IS IN TOWN

SEPTEMBER 18, 2008

Did you know that Williston has its very own Farmer Brown? Yup—when he's not growing students at UVM, Pat Brown grows rows and rows of gorgeous garlic. Temptress, Carpathian, Siberian, Leah, Georgia Fire, Romanian Red and Polish Hardneck are all thriving in picture perfect grids at the MacGregor Garlic Farm he shares with his wife, children's book author and illustrator, Amy Huntington.

Most cooks consider garlic a culinary rock star, but I never knew there were so many different bulbs grooving in Vermont until I ran into Farmer Brown at a food event. Pat shared samples of each variety and let me experiment with their different qualities.

The Georgia Fire is hot, but sultry, and salsas right through any fresh tomato dish with lots of style. The patrician Siberian is garlic royalty, with a purple skin and a common touch (use it in everything.) For a pure garlic splash, go with the Polish Hardneck. I like it chopped, swimming in a pool of cold pressed olive oil, smeared on lightly toasted artisanal bread, with a glass of Spanish Rioja acting as lifeguard. The zesty Carpathian is the stuff to ratchet up basic mashed potatoes along with buttermilk, melted butter and sea salt. Mellow out the Romanian Red by roasting it for puree—slice the head off, douse in olive oil, bake in a covered ramekin for 30 minutes at 350°F. It's great in my Garlic Flan recipe. Natural Provisions in Williston is now selling Farmer Brown's garlic varieties in limited quantities, so try some while they last.

ROASTED GARLIC FLAN

Preheat oven to 325°F. Scald 1–cup milk and 1–cup of cream in a saucepan; cool. In a work bowl whisk together 2–eggs and 2–additional egg yolks; ¼–cup of cooled roasted garlic puree; and a pinch of nutmeg. Whisk while slowly adding small amounts of the cream mixture to the eggs (tempering) to form a liquid custard; season with kosher salt and freshly ground pepper.

Lightly grease 4–ounce ramekins with cooking spray. Portion custard into ramekins and set ramekins into a large cake pan. Pullout oven rack and set pan on it. Fill the cake pan with boiling water until it hits half way up the ramekin to form a water bath (bain-marie). Cover with foil and gently slide into oven. Bake 32 minutes at 300°F or until flan is firm but glossy. Cool slightly; un-mold flan to serving plates. Top with a simple salsa of fresh tomatoes, parsley and basil. Serves 6.

Quick tips about garlic: There is no substitute for freshly chopped garlic. Choose heads with firm, plump bulbs and dry skins. Avoid garlic with sprouts—it's old and nasty. Try chopping cloves with a bit of kosher salt and the garlic will hold together nicely as the salt absorbs flavorful juices. Garlic presses are generally frowned upon because they are metal and react with the acid the garlic releases when pressed.

APPLE CRUMBLE RUMBLE

OCTOBER 7, 2008

It's autumn, and local orchards are busy harvesting a rumble of ruby Delicious, McIntosh, Empire, and Cortland apples. Crisp weather is the perfect time to get the gang out for a picking party, warm up the oven, and treat everybody to a fragrant, freshly baked pie. The easy Apple Crumble Pie topping makes for extra special eye appeal and texture. The pie requires only a bottom crust, which can be prepped a day ahead to save time. Serve slices of warm pie with generous chunks of Vermont cheddar cheese and maple walnut ice cream. Yummm—autumn never tasted so good!

APPLE CRUMBLE PIE

In a prep bowl combine 1 ½–cups white flour and a large pinch of salt. Add ½–cup Crisco shortening and blend with a fork until mixture is crumbly. Add 2–T of water and bind the mixture. If more water is needed, add slowly, in very light dribbles. Gather dough into a ball and wrap in plastic wrap, flatten into a disk, chill one hour. Roll out dough between 2 sheets of plastic wrap into a 14" round. Transfer dough to a 10" glass pie dish, fold overhang under. Crimp edges decoratively. Pierce bottom of crust all over with fork. Freeze crust 15 minutes (or up to 24 hours). Preheat oven to 375°F. Cover crust with pressed aluminum foil. Bake until golden and set 10 minutes. Cool.

APPLE FILLING

Peel, core, and thickly slice 5–pounds of any combination of McIntosh, Cortland, Empire and Delicious apples. Place apples in prep bowl and sprinkle 1–T fresh lemon juice over the apples. Melt 2–T of unsalted butter in non-stick pan over medium high heat. Stir in ½–cup of sugar, 1–t of cinnamon, and a pinch of clove. Add apples and sauté until coated and crisp–tender, about 3 minutes. Whisk together 2–T of apple cider and 1–T of cornstarch; add to apples and bring mixture to a boil, stirring constantly for 1 minute. Cool completely.

CRUMBLE TOPPING

In a prep bowl combine ¾–cup of white flour with ½–cup of sugar, ¼–cup packed brown sugar, 1–cup rolled oats, 6–T unsalted butter cut into small pieces, and a pinch of salt. Using clean fingertips, rub all ingredients together until moist clumps form. Place filling in pre-baked crust, sprinkle topping over apples. Bake at 375ºF until topping is golden brown, approximately 40–45 minutes.

CRASH COURSE AT THE MARKET

OCTOBER 16, 2008

Stocks are so cheap Wall Street is now called Wal-Mart Street, but for food shoppers, nothing looks like much of a bargain at the market. As always, it's nutritionally and economically best to eat what's in season, so this is the perfect time for a crash course on fall harvest vegetables. Squash, pumpkin, and root veggies such as carrot, celery root, rutabaga, parsnip, onion, and beet are perfection when roasted until caramelized. Loaded with natural sugars and ripe with earthy flavors, they substitute beautifully for meat in pasta, quesadillas, stews, and soups.

Eliminate cooking jitters by prepping ahead. Squash and pumpkin may look a little intimidating until you realize that all you have to do is split it down the middle, place it face-down on a parchment lined cookie sheet, and pop it into a 375°F oven until you can smell the sugars release, about an hour. Let it cool; use a fork to scrape the seeds away and harvest the flesh into a work bowl. Presto–maximum flavor with no peeling, chopping, or boiling. (Rinse and roast pumpkin seeds for a yummy snack).

To prep root vegetables, simply peel and cut into medium sized chunks, toss with a bit of olive oil and kosher salt, and roast for 45 minutes; turning occasionally. Any combination of root vegetables can be roasted together, but keep the beets separate, as the juices will stain a whole batch purple.

Here's an easy squash casserole that would make an excellent main dish; add a side of braised apple and kale, and a loaf of warm wholegrain bread.

CIDER-SPIKED SPAGHETTI SQUASH

Cut 1–large spaghetti squash into 4 quarters, and roast for 1 hour at 375ºF. Cool; scrape the flesh into a large prep bowl using a fork. (It really does look like spaghetti!) In a jar mix ½–cup apple cider; ¼–cup maple syrup; ½–t of powdered clove; 1–T of freshly minced ginger; 1–t kosher salt, and ½–t of red pepper flakes. Shake well. Pour over the squash mixing lightly.

Spray a 9x12" baking dish with vegetable spray. Pour in half of the squash mixture. Layer 6–ounces of provolone cheese over the squash; add the remaining squash. Bake at 350ºF for 30 minutes, uncovered. Top with breadcrumbs and bake until golden and bubbly, about 15 minutes.

BREAD CRUMBS

In a processor chop 3–cloves of garlic. Add 2–slices of whole wheat bread and pulse lightly until bread crumbles. Drizzle in a bit of olive oil and pulse 2–3 more times. Serves 8.

A LEG UP ON LAMB

OCTOBER 30, 2008

The weather is brisker and it's time to turn our merry-making indoors. For a cozy buffet, a grilled leg of lamb provides a stunning main attraction. I like to serve it with goat cheese scalloped potatoes, balsamic-glazed roasted beets, and maple butternut squash. For a quick herb-infused sauce to serve on the side, I simply strain and boil the lamb marinade and add a bit of crème fraiche.

This is Jeff Bradley's special, time-tested technique to grilling the somewhat unwieldy, yabba-dabba-doo, leg of lamb. The meat is grilled for exactly eleven minutes on each side in a closed, medium-hot grill. The lamb is then removed from the grill, and set to rest in sealed foil for 20 minutes and up to 2 hours. Because of the uneven terrain of a butterflied leg of lamb, this method yields a nicely charred exterior, and perfectly cooked slices in the rare to medium range—just enough variety to please the whole crowd.

What's the best part of this meal besides the show-stopping food? The all-important do-ahead factor: grilled lamb is resting while the side dishes are popped into the oven before guests even come through the door. The scene is a warm welcome, intoxicating aromas, and relaxed hosts—now that's a leg up on hospitality anytime of the year!

HERB MARINATED LEG OF LAMB

Order a 7–8 pound butterfly leg of lamb (the bone is removed.) Place lamb in a large non-metallic bowl or double encase 2 one-gallon Ziploc bags.

In a food processor mince 6–cloves of garlic. Microwave 1–8 oz. jar of mint jelly for 30 seconds; add to processor. Pulse 20 seconds. Add 2–T of olive oil; a fistful each of de-stemmed fresh rosemary and mint leaves; 1–cup of Dijon mustard; 3–T soy sauce; and generous pinches of kosher salt and freshly ground pepper. Process 60 seconds. Pour the marinade over the lamb. Marinate lamb for 1–3 days, flipping occasionally to incorporate the marinade.

Heat grill to medium-high, then lower to medium hot when ready to grill. Strain marinade into a saucepan and simmer over medium heat for at least 15 minutes. Stir in 4–ounces of crème fraiche, and adjust for seasoning. Pour into a gravy server.

Grill lamb for 11 minutes on each side, turning with tongs, for a total of 22 minutes maximum (trust me.) Place grilled meat in a double layer of heavy-duty aluminum foil lining a cookie sheet and seal tightly. Lamb must rest at least 20 minutes before carving and will hold up to 2 hours. Serves 10–12.

TEASERS FOR HOLIDAY APPETITES

NOVEMBER 13, 2008

The holidays are right around the corner, so it's time to perfect a few tasty teasers. Instead of throwing a full-fledged party this year (or, doing nothing at all) consider hosting what my Quebec-friend, Jen, calls *'Cinq à Sept'* (arrive at 5 and depart by 7). Stunning savories and a specialty drink are served, then guests move on to other engagements with appetites piqued. My hors d'oeuvres–retro with a twist—are hearty, healthy, and taste heavenly. Go ahead—give it a whirl, your friends will be pleased, the entertainment budget eased, and you can tease that you slaved all day.

BUBBLING BABY RUBENS

You'll need about 8–10 slices of Swiss cheese and 3–ounces of turkey pastrami. Lightly toast 8–slices of pumpernickel bread, crusts removed. Spread each slice of toast with whole grain Dijon mustard; cut each slice into quarters. Cut slices of Swiss cheese to match bread quarters and place one square on each quarter. Place on a baking sheet lined with parchment paper. Add 2 matching layers of turkey pastrami and one more square of Swiss cheese to each section. Slice each Ruben section in half again. Bake in a preheated 400°F oven until cheese is bubbling, about 4 minutes. Meanwhile, skewer 48–tiny gherkins (cornichons) with funky toothpicks. Pierce Ruben squares with the cornichons and plate. Makes 64.

SALMON STUDDED DEVILED EGGS

Prep 1–dozen hard-boiled eggs, preferably organic. (Tip: boil eggs with one–third cup salt and cool completely for easier peeling.) Gently combine 6–ounces of chopped smoked salmon (look for salmon 'trim' in seafood freezer section); 1–T baby capers; ⅓–cup chopped fresh dill, ⅓–cup finely minced red onion; ⅓–cup (or less) mayonnaise; kosher salt and freshly ground pepper to taste. Split each cooked egg length-wise and remove yolks. Crumble six whole yolks into salmon mixture and mix lightly in with a fork. Loosely dollop small portions into individual egg white halves. Garnish with a sprinkle of paprika and a wisp of dill. Makes 24.

PERUVIAN PURPLES WITH CAVIAR

Cut 12–small Peruvian purple potatoes in half. Place potatoes in a wide sauté pan and cover with cold water and 1–T of salt; don't crowd potatoes. Bring to a boil, then reduce heat and simmer 7–9 minutes until potatoes are just barely tender. Gently transfer a paper towel-lined baking sheet and cool. Whisk together ½–cup of low-fat sour cream, mayo, OR cream fraiche with some drained horseradish (to taste), and kosher salt and pepper. Chill. Arrange potatoes on a serving platter and spoon a tiny dollop of cream onto each potato. Top with a pinch of black caviar and then add a small "X" cross of fresh chive over each potato top. Makes 24.

JUST SAY NO TO JELLY BELLY

DECEMBER 10, 2008

Would you like to forego that 'bowl full of jelly' feeling come Hanukah-Christmas-Kwanza morning? Then don't succumb to the seasonal eating mentality of "to hell with it, I'll start after the holidays." Now is the time to recommit to healthy lifestyle choices, even as we fa-la-la-la our way through the kitchen spreading joy and peanut brittle. This means regular cardio and core exercise, lots of water, and whole foods rich in nutrients and low in fat and sugar. (A nap-for-no-reason is also a good idea.)

I'm no food-Scrooge and plan to indulge at parties, but making mindful choices to balance each day is the best present I can give myself, and my family. For a quick and healthy meal nothing beats freshly toasted quesadillas on Joseph's flax and oat bran tortillas; load them with black beans, brown rice, lots of wilted fresh spinach, and a bit of cheese or lean protein. I also love the Fage brand of Greek-style yogurt. The 0% fat container is 8–ounces and 90 calories of dreamy cream and it's readily available at supermarkets. The mouth-feel is so rich I can eat one for lunch and feel completely satisfied (unlike other yogurts that leave me feeling like I just got a lump of coal in my stocking.) The yogurt is delicious on a baked sweet potato with steamed broccoli, or as a topping for fresh fruit.

Planning ahead for hunger pains is a huge factor in making smart choices. I always keep a small bag of trail mix in my car, along with Minneola's or grapes, and cans of V8 juice and water. These items come in really handy when I'm busy running errands and need a quick fix. One of my most successful seasonal tricks is a spicy vegan cookie that is loaded with the good stuff, yet tastes like a holiday treat. Try one with a steaming mug of coffee to super-fuel your mornings or late afternoons—it's the essence of guilt-free luxury. I want to wish all of my wonderful readers good luck with their holiday preparations, enjoy every moment of this precious season. And each time you belly laugh with joy—may it be with abs of steel.

VEGAN POWER COOKIES

Preheat oven to 375°F. In a large mixing bowl combine the following with a wooden spoon: 29–ounces of canned pumpkin (not prepared pie filling); ½–cup canola oil; 2–ripe mashed bananas; ¾–cup brown sugar; ½–cup molasses; 1–T vanilla; ½–t, each, ginger and cinnamon; 1–t cloves; 1 ½–cups ground flaxseed meal (or wheat germ); 2–t baking soda; ¾–cup tiny carob chips (or chocolate chips); ¾–cup dried cranberries and blueberry mix; ¾–cup shredded coconut; and ¾–cup crushed walnuts. Fold in without over mixing: 3–cups old-fashioned style oats; and 4–cups whole-wheat flour.

Dollop cookies onto 4 parchment-lined baking sheets, makes 30 cookies. Bake 18 minutes. Cool. Freeze in small batches until ready for use.

WHAT I REMEMBERED THIS YEAR

DECEMBER 25, 2008

There has been an alarming increase in the things I know nothing about. It seems the more I learn about food and cooking the more I realize how little I know. And now that I've seen the other side of fifty, the little bit I know, I can't always remember when I need it. I hate my brain.

At least I remembered to keep notes for this column—little tips and techniques that helped to make me a better eater and cook in 2008. I'm sharing these morsels in the hopes that somebody out there will help me to remember them, and treat me someday with a sweet kernel of knowledge.

First, a subject near and dear to my waistline: the ultimate chocolate chip cookie. This past summer the *New York Times* revealed the critical element to creating truly epic chocolate chips cookies (7/09/08). In the interest of sound reporting, I experimented–several times, in fact–and concur with their findings. The dough is markedly more complex and delicious (with a finer crumb) when refrigerated 24 to 36 hours prior to baking.

A burlesque of happiness: perfectly poached eggs smashed over crispy French fries, (Don't forget the sea salt.)

Shrimp: My favorite food now gets a sprinkle of sugar before searing in a pan of hot olive oil. Why? The shrimp quickly turn a gorgeous copper color, while remaining plump and succulent. How come? The Maillard Reaction, the chemical reaction between a protein and a reducing sugar in heat. (It's the same thing that happens when you make toast.)

I feverently wish that it weren't true, but it's a fact: as baby boomers age, not only does the memory fade, but so do the taste buds. Yikes! Can pureed prunes be in my near future? Don't panic, the food industry is on the taste case—it's no coincidence there are so many spicy rubs and salsas on menus today. At home, try using red pepper flakes instead of ground pepper in recipes. I use a 1:4 ratio when substituting the hot stuff.

The paradox of globalization: I went half way around the world to eat authentic Lebanese food this summer, and discovered that my childhood auntie, Sandy O'Brien, cooks it better.

Remember: Seek out ethnic flavors right in your own town. There are great cooks just waiting to share their taste treasures with your adventurous palate.

2009

HAIL TO THE BEEF

JANUARY 15, 2009

President Obama's historic inauguration will take place January 20, 2009. To celebrate, I'm preparing the best dish I ate last year (thanks to my neighbor, Shona Lothrop.) *Individual Beef Wellingtons* with Mushrooms, Spinach, and Blue Cheese is adapted from a recipe in *Fine Cooking*. Cheers!

SUNDAY: PREP

Slice 8–ounces of crimini mushrooms and sauté for 15 minutes in 1-T of hot olive oil. Deglaze with ¼–cup dry sherry, cooking until all liquid evaporates. Stir in 2–cloves of minced garlic, and ½–t, each, fresh thyme leaves and chopped fresh rosemary.

Repeat process with 2–thinly sliced medium onions, deglazing and cooking until caramelized and dry. Combine the batch and season with coarse salt and freshly ground black pepper. Chill.

Microwave 12–ounces of fresh baby spinach; squeeze in a paper towel to dry. Wrap in fresh paper towel and place in a small bowl. Slice 4 1–ounce slabs of Maytag blue cheese. Chill ingredients.

Sear 4–portions of seasoned beef tenderloin, 6–ounces each, in hot olive oil for 2 minutes on each side. Chill.

MONDAY: ASSEMBLE WELLINGTONS

Thaw 2–sheets (1–pound) frozen puff pastry, Pepperidge Farm brand, for 20 minutes. Be sure the pastry is pliable enough to unfold without breaking. Place each sheet onto individual sheets of parchment paper and roll out to two 14x17" rectangles. Slice each rectangle on the diagonal, creating a total of 4–triangles.

Working quickly, stack spinach, cheese, beef, and the mushroom mixture into center of each pastry triangle. (Use a slotted spoon for the mushroom mixture to eliminate excess liquid.)

Seal the panels together by pulling up sides and pinching each together where the panels meet. Place bundle, sealed side down, on a sheet lined with parchment that fits into your freezer. Don't worry if the package doesn't look gorgeous, it's more important that it's well sealed so the juices don't leak out. Using a pastry brush, seal the packets with an egg wash mix of 1–egg; and 1–t of water. Freeze bundles.

TUESDAY: ROAST WELLINGTONS

Heat oven to 400ºF. Make another egg wash. Remove the Wellingtons from the freezer (do not thaw) and brush them with a fresh coat of egg wash. Put them on a lightly greased rimmed heavy baking sheet and roast 20 minutes. Reduce the heat to 350°F and cook until the internal temperature is 110°F (be sure the tip of the thermometer is inserted in the center of the package), another 35 minutes. Serves 4.

SCARE WINTER BLUES AWAY

FEBRUARY 26, 2009

Yes, the light is changing and the days are getting longer, but a harsh fact of northern living is that we still have a lot of winter to go. What can we purchase in the produce department to perk up our spirits as we whittle our waistlines waiting for spring? How about making friends with that scary, hairy softball knob, celery root? This is my favorite winter vegetable and it suffers, rightly so, from a beauty-and-the-beast syndrome. I'll admit that it is downright frightening to plop that monster into your grocery cart, but give it a chance, Belle, you'll be glad you did.

After peeling away the skin of the celery root (also called celeriac) you'll reveal something that looks like a potato. Shred it raw in a food processor or grate it by hand—you'll be rewarded with ribbons of snow white, crunchy, fresh tasting slaw. Mixed with lemon aioli and flat-leafed parsley, you can practically taste spring coming around the corner. Lemony Celeriac Salad pairs beautifully with late winter braised meats as well as lighter entrees such as grilled salmon.

LEMONY CELERIAC SALAD

Peel one hearty knob of celery root, shred it, and place in a prep bowl.

Lemon aioli: in a small processor, finely mince 4–garlic cloves and the zest of one lemon. Add 1–heaping T of Dijon mustard, the juice of the zested lemon, and 1–cup of Hellmann's mayo. Process 30 seconds. Add kosher salt and fresh pepper to taste.

Lightly fold the lemon aioli over the celery root. Top with several handfuls of clean, dry, de-stemmed flat leaf parsley. Serve immediately, or cover with plastic and store in fridge. Salad can be made up to one day ahead; serves 8.

WARM SPINACH SALAD

Another veggie combination is a warm salad of fresh spinach and Brussels sprouts. A savory side, it is superb with steak or chicken or just a bit of bacon.

Prep 15–20 Brussels sprouts by slicing off each bottom and peeling a few layers of leaf off. Place in a glass bowl, cover, and microwave for 3 minutes on high (do ahead). In a large sauté pan, toast 2–ounces of walnuts for 40 seconds; reserve in a small bowl. When cool, gently break up the walnuts by hand.

Add 1–T of butter to a hot sauté pan and lightly brown the butter. Add the Brussels sprouts; cover and sear for 2 minutes, shaking pan often. Add 4–generous handfuls of fresh spinach; cover and turn off the heat. Set for 5 minutes, until spinach is wilted. Place in a serving dish and top with sea salt, fresh pepper, walnuts, and crumbled blue cheese. Serves 4; doubles nicely.

RECESSION LESSONS

MARCH 26, 2009

The crashing economy presents a unique shop-portunity to score more bang for our nutritional buck at the supermarket. While downgrading the quality of our food is never the way to go, reviewing a few shopping and eating lessons can make a big difference to our waistlines and bottom lines.

First and foremost, do your homework. Study supermarket circulars to spot weekly deals and learn the prices of staple items for comparison. Next, make a strategic shopping list: list general sections of the store and plug needed items in by section. On the reverse side, sketch out the week's meal plan. Planning provides focus, reduces impulse purchasing, and ensures that you have all the ingredients you need for the entire week. No more multiple trips for forgotten items (this is what really jacks up the food budget.)

Buy food in a natural state whenever possible. While overly processed packaged foods are always more expensive, coupons are a smart way to load up on healthy non-perishables like canned beans, pasta sauce, whole-wheat pasta, and tuna. A stockpile ensures that nutritious food is always available, and a quick, home-cooked meal is only fifteen minutes away.

Don't forget to shop at ethnic and farmer's markets. They have amazing produce that is cheaper and nicer than the supermarket. They also sell unique bottled sauces and cooking condiments below retail prices of stores. Always buy what's in season and branch out of your culinary comfort zone by experimenting with new varieties of veggies.

Fruit is a challenge this time of year: so expensive, big carbon footprint, yet it's vital to our wellbeing. Invest in citrus fruits that pack well in lunches; homemade applesauce is always a hit for snacks or dessert. I splurge on honeydew melon and black grapes to prep containers of fruit salad for workdays.

Penny-wise is pound goulash: don't buy cheap bulk stuff you don't really want to eat. You'll end up tortured by palate-numbing meals you hate, squashing any inclination to stay on a healthy nutritional track. Rather, invest in smaller amounts of quality foods that satisfy you and keep you enthusiastic about mealtimes. (This is how the French manage to eat well yet stay slim.) For example, to trim your meat budget, eat pork or chicken sparingly–as a condiment with grains or rice—rather than as a main course.

I've said it before, and I'll say it again: invest in an electric rice cooker. Aromatic steel-cut oatmeal is ready to eat when you wake up in the morning; a healthy brown rice stew perfumes the air as you walk in the door for dinner; and it even works as a mini-crockpot for braising cheaper cuts of meat. Now, that's what I call a bargain.

THE GANG OF NINE

APRIL 9, 2009

I recently had the pleasure of sharing Asian cooking techniques with a Williston group that will be known to my readers only as "The Gang of 9". Did I use good judgment serving Asian I.V. cocktails (vodka spiked with fresh ginger juice, Rose's lime juice, and mint) before they began wielding the knives? You bet. They performed like seasoned Peking Acrobats in a kitchen choreography rivaling any Iron Chef competition. We managed to turn out a pretty platter or two, mastering Healthy Pork Fried Rice and Siren Shrimp with Bok Choy. The Chinese Chicken Salad was a big hit, as well. We think it's the perfect spring dish for a potluck party, grand luncheon, or weekend family treat.

CHINESE CHICKEN SALAD

On a gentle simmer, poach 4–chicken breasts in 4–cups of chicken stock until tender, about 15 minutes. Cool the chicken and then slice breasts into bite-sizes cubes; reserve.

Combine ½–cup soy sauce, ¼–cup sesame oil, and ¼–cup rice wine vinegar in a large prep bowl. In a large pot, boil 24–ounces of fettuccini noodles for 10 minutes; strain. Pour pasta into the prep bowl and coat the noodles; reserve.

Salad: 1–package of matchstick carrots; 1–package of ramen noodles, lightly crumbled; 1–cup slivered almonds, toasted; 12–ounces of fresh bean sprouts; 3–cups fresh pea pods, sliced in half; 1–Napa cabbage thinly sliced across the grain, forming a pile of thin ringlets. Toss all of these ingredients into a large prep bowl, reserve.

Dressing: In a food processor, mince together a 3"–piece of freshly peeled ginger; 4–garlic cloves; and the zest of a large orange. Add ½–cup of Tahini; 2–T of Dijon mustard; 1–cup soy sauce; ½–cup sherry; ¼–cup fish sauce; 4–T of chili garlic sauce; and ½–cup brown sugar. Blend well; thin with additional orange juice if necessary.

Combine the chicken and noodles; coat with some of the dressing. Gently fold in veggie mixture and turn the salad onto a large platter. Drizzle remaining dressing over the top. Garnish with fresh pea shoots. Serve immediately, using tongs, or cover and refrigerate up to two hours. Serves 12–14.

WOK YOUR TALK

APRIL 23, 2009

As a nation, we talk skinny but we eat fat. Who among us has not indulged the paradox of serving up greasy, tasteless Chinese take-out and calling it a family treat? As the spring break draws to a close, why not gather the gang, dust off the wok, and whip up a savory specialty everyone can brag about: Healthy Ginger Fried Rice. The rice is loaded with fiber and fresh veggies, and the protein works as a condiment rather than the main feature. Any combination of pork, shrimp, chicken, tofu, and scrambled eggs works just fine. While not strictly Asian, the asparagus gives the rice a nice springtime perk. I like to use Lundberg Wild Rice Country Blend brown rice, but basmati or jasmine works well, too (then you can call it "Princess Jasmine Fried Rice".)

HEALTHY GINGER FRIED RICE

Rice: prep ahead. Measure 5–cups of Lundberg Wild Rice Country Blend and cook in a rice cooker, or steam rice in a closely watched pot. Place cooked rice into a large prep bowl. (Let the kids stir it with a chopstick.)

Veggie Prep: chop 2–large onions; dice 3–cups baby carrots; slice 6–stalks of celery; seed and dice 3–large bell peppers: red, orange, and yellow. Slice a large bunch of asparagus into bite-sized pieces.

Reserve Veggies (set aside for later): 2–cans water chestnuts, drained and chopped; one 12–ounce bag of fresh bean sprouts; and 2–cups frozen peas, thawed.

Final Topping: Thinly slice 6–scallions; slice 1–head of bok choy widthwise into thin ribbon slices.

Protein Prep: Dice bite-sized chunks of roasted pork, chicken, or shrimp to make 3–cups. Scramble 3–eggs, chop up mass, cool.

Dressing Prep: (Do this while veggies sizzle in the wok.) In a food processor mince 6–large garlic cloves along with a 3" hunk of peeled fresh ginger. Add 1–cup soy sauce, ½–cup orange juice, 2–T sesame oil, and 2–T of chili garlic sauce. Process 1 minute.

In a hot wok or large sauté pan, heat 2–T of peanut oil. Add onion and carrot and sauté for 10 minutes; season lightly with kosher salt, layering flavors with each veggie. Add celery, and cook 5 minutes more. Add peppers, cooking 5 minutes more. Add asparagus and protein for a final 2 minutes.

Deglaze the wok with 6–ounces of sherry. Add the cooked veggies to the rice. Add the reserved veggies. Pour dressing over rice, gently folding ingredients together. Place on serving platter and top with scallions and ribbons of bok choy. Makes 12–14 servings; the rice reheats beautifully.

ALL A-TWITTER ON MOTHER'S DAY

MAY 7, 2009

My darling daughters won't be home for Mother's Day, so I'm planning an "ambient awareness" holiday. I'll send Twitter updates hourly, just so they'll know my every move, all day long (nothing like a little mother-daughter bonding between Vermont, Egypt, and Oregon.) Then, I'll add to my status on Facebook with photos of me gardening. At the appointed hour we'll share some face time via Skype and I can tell them all about my sore back and how the pugs peed on the new carpet. Later, we can exchange some random voicemails, and I'll even text a photo or two of our garage cleanup project. This should keep us all in the family loop—a fascinating day of breaking news.

If I could actually see the tiny keypad on my cell phone I would text the girls our menu for tonight: a chopped spring salad, herbed rice pilaf, juicy grilled steak and shrimp kabobs, and individual trifle puddings. (Oops, I forgot! They can see it on my website). Frankly, I would happily trade all the world's modern satellite capability to have my daughters seated around the dinner table sharing some real-time bickering and hugs. If you're lucky enough to have loved ones joining you for Mother's Day, hold them close and then head for the kitchen—everyone can pitch in to make this easy, excellent feast. It will be ready in under an hour (especially if you limit the Twitter updates).

CHOPPED SPRING SALAD

Fry 4–ounces of cubed pancetta and reserve. Chop one head of endive, radicchio and Boston Bibb lettuce each. Chop up a bulb of fresh fennel. Snap the base off of a bundle of asparagus spears and rough chop the stalks. Thinly slice a small red onion. Mix pancetta together with veggies in a salad bowl. In a small covered jar combine ½–cup olive oil; ¼–cup best quality balsamic vinegar; a pinch of ginger; dry mustard; kosher salt; and fresh pepper; shake vigorously. Lightly dress salad with clean hands. Crumble 4–ounces of Point Reyes blue cheese over the salad. Serves 4, doubles easily.

HERBED RICE PILAF

Follow directions on 1–2 boxes and top with a handful of freshly chopped chives and tarragon before serving. Serves 4–8.

STRAWBERRY MINI-TRIFLES

In a bowl whisk 16–ounces of Fage Greek 0% fat yogurt, with one 8–ounce container of Cool Whip, and 1–T of vanilla and sugar each. In 4 festive wine or parfait glasses alternately layer sliced strawberries, crumbled chocolate covered macaroons (store-bought) with the yogurt mixture to make 4 desserts. Chill 1–2 hours. Doubles easily.

THE SAVVY SHOPPER

JUNE 4, 2009

I finally got around to reading Marion Nestle's book *What to Eat: An Aisle-by-Aisle Guide to Savvy Food Choices and Good Eating.* I wish I hadn't waited so long! Nestle, a professor of nutrition at NYU, has filled her book with practical shopping tips supported by sound science and good common sense.

In a perverse twist of fate, our opportunity to buy more organic foods is expanding just as food budgets are shrinking, so I was especially interested in what Nestle had to say about savvy strategies for the careful eater. Environmental and nutritional research has determined that by purchasing organic food from the list of the top most contaminated produce, you can reduce toxic exposure by upwards of 90%. This mean you can take the worry out of choices and save money purchasing local, sustainable, and traditional versions of the least contaminated fruits and veggies.

"Certified organic" means that the US Department of Agriculture (ams.USDA.gov) has inspected the producer to ensure that they are not using fertilizers or pesticides in the growing process (organicconsumers.org). "Sustainable" means produce is grown in a scientific process designed to improve the quality of the soil and reduce wasteful energy practices. (John Adams, of our local Adams Farm Market, does a laudable job with this process and is a fountain of knowledge.) "Local" means that the food was grown within a loose 100–mile radius of your home (localharvest.org). "Traditional" food is mass-produced and shipped from production centers all over the globe (supermarkets).

The general rule of thumb is if you are going to eat the skin of a fruit or vegetable, opt for organic or sustainable local produce. Here is a list of guidelines for your shopping list:

Organic Preferred List: Apples, Cherries, Celery, Cucumbers, Imported Grapes, Herbs, Lettuce, Nectarines, Peaches, Pears, Potatoes, Spinach, Strawberries, and Sweet Bell Peppers (I'm going to add eggs and dairy products to this list.)

Sustainable/Local/Traditional List: Asparagus, Avocados, Bananas, Blueberries, Broccoli, Cabbage, Eggplant, Fresh or Frozen Sweet Corn and Peas, Green Beans, Kiwis, Mangoes, Mellon, Onions, Papayas, Pineapples, Raspberries and Squash.

The savvy shopper will use all four sources to create healthy meals that still honor the family budget. For example, traditional flash-frozen vegetables are far superior in quality, and cheap, compared with some of the exhausted trucked-in organic produce. Tomatoes, ideally purchased and eaten only in season, just taste better if they are local. Organic, sustainable, and local foods are now coming into their peak season as farm markets abound with stellar stuff; it's prime time for bargain shopping and superb eating.

THE CRUMBLE JUMBLE

JULY 7, 2009

All cooks have a couple of foods they obsess about. I have an open rendezvous with any decent scalloped potato recipe that comes down the pipe; and I'll admit that I think more about streusel toppings than I do about the crumbling economy.

European streusel, or "crumble" as we Yanks like to call it, is the love child of a piecrust and a cookie. Quite simply, it is better than either: you get the crunchy satisfaction of a decadent dessert with out all of the hidden calories. I have spent the past year or so puzzling out the perfect crumble topping just to be ready for berry season. This recipe works well with almost any combination of fresh fruit: blueberries, black berries, freshly pitted cherries, strawberries, raspberries, peaches, nectarines, and even diced rhubarb. Use a baking dish that is not too deep, with plenty of surface, so the beloved crumble topping can shine. This is a great dessert for Fourth of July festivities—it's a cinch to make, and your friends will be obsessing about it for days afterward.

BERRY JUMBLE CRUMBLE

Preheat oven to 375ºF. Prep 8–10 cups of fresh berries and stone fruit and place in a large bowl. Sprinkle ½–cup of sugar and 1–T of lemon juice over fruit, fold gently with a spatula. Sprinkle 3–T of flour over fruit.

Cover a 9x12" baking dish with non-stick spray and add the fruit. Bake for 20 minutes.

Prepare the crumble topping by peeling the zest off of a large lemon and mincing it in the large bowl of a food processor. Add a pinch of salt; 1–cup of flour, ½–cup of sugar, and pulse to blend. With on/off turns, slowly add 4–ounces) of cold butter, that has been cut into smaller cubes, until coarse crumbs form. Add 1–cup of walnuts and 1–cup of oats and pulse on/off for 15 seconds. Add 1–T of whole milk and do quick pulses until the mixture is clumpy-looking, about 10–15 seconds

Top the fruit with the crumble, scattering loosely over the surface. (Do not handle the crumble too much!) Bake for 25 minutes until the topping is a yummy golden and the fruit bubbles out the sides. Since there is no bottom crust, splurge and serve it with a dollop of vanilla ice cream or frozen yogurt, and top with a sprig of fresh mint.

THE CHEESE WHIZ

AUGUST 27, 2009

I spent last weekend cheesing my way to a potential heart attack. First, I saw the delightful movie *Julie and Julia*, a must see that is enhanced by smuggling in a wedge of ripe Brie and a crisp Bourgogne white. After the movie, I sated my lust for French food at a local café: buttery escargots, paté de champagne, fromage de chèvre grille, and fresh sardines did the trick.

Still breathing, my next event was a super cheese-studded party to celebrate Vermont Butter and Cheese Company's twenty-five years in business. There were kudos and cheese curds flying around this festive reunion as slices of baguette, smeared with hand crafted Bonne Bouche, Coupole and Bijou chèvres, paraded on trays just begging me to pick them off, which I happily did. The Vermont Butter and Cheese Company is largely credited for creating the specialty cheese industry in Vermont and has won hundreds of blue ribbons in international competitions.

I spent the next day cheesing it up at the Vermont Cheesemakers Festival at Shelburne Farms (vtcheesefest.com). Dozens of Vermont artisanal cheese makers shared over one hundred varieties of hand made cow and sheep milk cheeses; my favorite of the day was Cabot Clothbound Cheddar from Jasper Hill Farm, Greensboro, Vermont. I enjoyed a demonstration of cheese making and tasting by French native Marc Druart and cheese writer Max McCalman of NYC's Artisanal restaurants. Another session was a sensory paring of five cheeses with bacon and chocolate; pumpkin and caraway; salt, oil and honey; cranberry compote and pickled beets; dilly green beans and tomato; and cider butter with maple crunch popcorn. Try it sometime—crazy fun on the plate and on the palate. I was too cheesed out to handle the wine and beer parings, but they sure looked appealing.

The festival was held in partnership with UVM's cheese education program, the Vermont Institute for Artisanal Cheese, which provides weeklong classes in cheese techniques for anyone interested in cheese making as a hobby or possible business. The guest instructors are experts from all over the world.

This week I'll be jogging around town munching rolls of Tums and rabbit food from my local farmer's market. I can handle this regime as long as there is still a smidgeon of Chocolate Apple Mascarpone Cheesecake leftover in my fridge to bridge the gap. The recipe is available at butterandcheese.net.

HALLOWEEN HOOT

OCTOBER 22, 2009

This the season for pumpkins, spice, and everything sugar. Why not make some sweet memories by whipping up a batch of homemade cupcakes? These recipes are simple and fun for any age. The pumpkin cupcakes are milder and will appeal to the little goblins on your watch, while the carrot cake cupcakes please the child in all of us. Your kitchen will smell wonderful and your party platter will be ready to rock. A word of caution: take it easy on the cream cheese frosting if you are planning to go as Elvis or the French Maid this year.

PUMPKIN CUPCAKES

Preheat oven to 350°F. In a large bowl use a wooden spoon to combine 4–eggs; ¾–cup canola oil; 2–cups sugar; 16–ounces of canned pumpkin; a pinch of salt; 3–t cinnamon; 1–t baking soda; and 1–t baking powder.

Add 2–cups white flour and stir to combine. Pour batter into cupcake molds (lined with paper cups) two-thirds full; bake at 350°F for 18–20 minutes, or until cake tester comes out clean. Makes 24 cakes.

CARROT SPICE CUPCAKES

Preheat oven to 350°F. In a large bowl use a wooden spoon to combine dry ingredients: 2–cups flour; 2–cups sugar; 2–t baking powder; 2–t baking soda; 1–t salt; 2–t of cinnamon; 2–t of cloves.

Stir in 1–cup vegetable oil; 3–cups grated carrots; 1–cup coconut; 4–eggs; ½–cup of chopped walnuts and or raisins (optional.) Pour batter into cupcake molds (lined with paper cups) two–thirds full; bake at 350°F for 25–30 minutes, or until cake tester comes out clean. Makes 24 cakes.

CREAM CHEESE FROSTING

With an electric mixer, beat together 8–ounces of lite cream cheese and 8–ounces of unsalted butter (room temperature) and 2–t vanilla or almond extract. Slowly add 1–cup of confectionary sugar (adding more or less sugar for sweetness and volume desired). Beat until smooth. Cool frosting in fridge 20 minutes before using. Generously frost tops of cooled cupcakes; decorate with candy pumpkins and candy corn.

THANKS-GIVING PIG-OUT

NOVEMBER 19, 2009

Want to blow your collective family gathering away this year at the Thanksgiving table? Serve praline bacon on anything–anything at all—and they will go berzerk. This bacon is more than just a trendy kiss from hog heaven—in my kitchen it is already a tradition.

I know it's shameful, but I have always found the traditional Thanksgiving menu a bit lackluster; now that there is going to be a little pork-action at the table, I'll be much happier. Praline bacon freezes well, so do it ahead and dole your stash out like a crack addict. This holiday I am torn between embedding precious chunks among roasted sweet potatoes, or topping creamy cheddar crackers with it. Maybe I'll do both—after all, Thanksgiving is the official pig-out.

PRALINE BACON (FROM CHEF ROBIN SCHEMPP)

Preheat oven to 350°F. In a wide, shallow dish combine 1–cup brown sugar; ½–cup roughly ground almonds/pecans; 2–t dry mustard; 1 ½–T of coarse ground pepper; 1–t kosher salt; ⅓–cup mustard seeds.

Separate 2–pounds of bacon into individual strips. Dip and press each slice into the sugar mixture on both sides. Lay bacon strips on a large, rimmed baking sheet covered with parchment. Sprinkle excess sugar mixture over the bacon slices in the pan. Roast the bacon until fat begins to render, about 6 minutes. Rotate the pan front–to-back and continue roasting until the bacon is crisp and brown, 8 minutes. Cool; cut bacon into bite-sized pieces.

SWEET POTATOES

Peel and chunk-cut desired amount of sweet potatoes. Toss potatoes in a bit of olive oil and sprinkle with kosher salt. Roast at 400°F for 45 minutes; gently flip the batch halfway through cooking for even roasting. Pour potatoes into a serving bowl and stud with lots of praline bacon.

CHEDDAR CHEESE HORS D'OEUVRES

In the bowl of a food processor, chop 1–pound of very sharp white Cheddar cheese. Add 3–T of milk and pulse until the mixture forms a creamy paste. Meanwhile, caramelized apples by sautéing 5 peeled and chopped apples in 1–T of butter until soft (but not mushy.) Spread Cheddar on a plain rice cracker; add a layer of apple, top with a chunk of praline bacon.

2010

FIRE & ICE

JANUARY 7, 2010

My Bikram yoga teacher, Kelly, ends class with a rift on Aristotle: "everything in moderation, even moderation." During the past holiday season I followed her wisdom carefully, and while I've enjoyed every morsel of my chocolate macaroons, rare roast beef, and lobster mac 'n cheese (all in moderation, of course) I'm now hot to detox from the flow of artery clogging foods.

During the frigid month of January, more robust vegetarian dishes will be bubbling on my stove. Some will feature lentils, barley and wild rice, while others showcase pasta and polenta. All of them will have lots of spice, heat, cheese, and vegetables—roasted, sautéed, and pureed—to crank up the nutritional value of each dish.

To ward off icy evenings, introduce a little fire to your belly with this moderately spicy pureed pasta sauce. It is loaded with health enhancing garlic, onion, orange zest, and rosemary; the mushrooms and Parmesan 'meat bits' provide umami—the flavor that transforms a basic dish into a truly satisfying meal.

RED PEPPER & PARMESAN PASTA

Heat 1–T of olive oil in a large sauté pan. Rough chop two sweet onions and add to the pan. Sauté 15 minutes. Add 6–minced garlic cloves. Deglaze the pan with ½–cup of hearty red wine or stock, scraping up browned bits. Mince the zest of one small orange and ¼–cup of fresh rosemary leaves. Add to sauté pan.

Add 1–28 ounce can of crushed tomatoes, ½–cup orange juice; ¼–cup vodka; and 1–12 ounce jar of roasted red peppers, drained and rough chopped. Cut a palm-sized hunk off of a Parmesan cheese block (include the rind) and add to sauce. Add two pinches of kosher salt and slightly less than ¼–t of red pepper flakes. Cover and simmer on low 20–30 minutes until cheese is pliable.

Meanwhile, slice 10–ounces of Crimini mushrooms and sauté in 1–T of olive oil for 20 minutes; reserve.

Remove Parmesan chunk from sauce and cut into small, soft bites; reserve. Puree sauce until smooth. Add the mushrooms and Parmesan bites, and 1–T of cream. While gently reheating, adjust for seasonings and pepper heat. Serve over whole-wheat pasta; serves 4–6.

RUBE GOLDBERG RECIPES

JANUARY 21, 2010

Take a complex set of instructions and make it simple; by virtue of space allotment, that's my job every column. Since I cannot properly follow a real recipe, my creations are safe from the copyright police, yet there are always ethics and etiquette to consider when adapting a recipe. The guidelines of the International Association of Culinary Professionals focus on giving proper attribution to recipes that are published or taught. Using the words "adapted from," or "based on," depending on how much a recipe has been revised, is protocol.

The only time a recipe should be printed without attribution is when it has been changed so substantially that it no longer resembles its source. In culinary school we learned that if three elements of the recipe are changed, then it has evolved to a new recipe. Because cooking is as much invention as art, universal participation dictates that recipes are always evolving. It is the sum of a cook's knowledge, preference for technique, adaptability, and quality of ingredients.

Reader Nancy Suarez shared this recipe. Not only is it a delicious soup, but an excellent example of an evolved recipe. Nancy wrote, "My husband, Joe, found this many years ago in Bon Appetit, we have modified it to be vegetarian."

Looking at the first version, their adaptation is truly a simpler, original recipe.

WILD RICE SOUP SUAREZ

On medium-low, heat a soup pot with 2–T of olive oil. Sauté 1–chopped onion; 3–stalks of chopped celery; 2–chopped carrots; 5–sliced Crimini mushrooms; and 1–t chopped garlic in until soft, about 10–15 minutes. Add 1 ⅓–cups of wild rice (or a blend of rice); stir to coat. Add 7–cups of water; 3–Knorr vegetable bouillon cubes (double size/strength); and 1–bay leaf.

Simmer, with pot partially covered, until rice is tender, stirring occasionally, about 1 hour. Remove bay leaf. Puree 2–cups of the soup batch in a processor and return it to the pot; alternatively, use an immersion blender for 30 seconds. To finish, gently reheat soup stirring in ½–cup of whipping cream or half & half; season with salt and pepper to taste. Serves 8.

IT'S NOT COMPLICATED

MARCH 4, 2010

Oscar fever is at full pitch this week. Two of my favorite movies this past year involve Meryl Streep and food. In *Julie & Julia*, Streep reincarnates the cooking icon Julia Child with the grace and precision of an avatar. And I'm still salivating over her role as Jane in *It's Complicated*. The kitchen and restaurant scenes, along with the sheer artistry of the casseroles and confections, made me weak with hunger and envy.

It's reassuring to know that movie food is styled with glycerin and glue, rendering it gorgeous but inedible, and that whipping up attractive, great tasting food on your own is NOT complicated. With spring festivities just around the corner here are two recipes that will help you to create professional looking food that will thrill your very own fan base.

BOOM-BOOM'S MACAROONS

Mix together 14–ounces of sweetened coconut; 14–ounces of unsweetened coconut; 1–14 ounce can of non-fat condensed milk, ¼–teaspoon of almond and vanilla extract, each; and 1–cup toasted chopped almonds (optional). Mix well and shape into 20 flat bottomed-ovals. Place on a cookie sheet and bake at 350°F for 15 minutes.

Microwave 2–cups of chocolate chips for 45 seconds; stir in 2–t of canola oil.

On a fresh cookie sheet lined with parchment paper drop a 1–t of chocolate into a pool and gently press a macaroon on it, creating a chocolate base. Repeat; drizzle a little chocolate over each top. Macaroons freeze beautifully.

SPRINGTIME ASPARAGUS

Buy a big bunch of fat-fingered asparagus and remove bottom stems by snapping their tough bases. Toss spears in a little olive oil. Fire up the grill and roast the asparagus spears until they blister and glisten, about 5 minutes.

Place asparagus on a platter and scatter sea salt and fresh pepper over all. Serve a Rouille-styled mayonnaise on the side: chop 4–garlic cloves and a big bunch of mint leaves in a mini-processor. Add 2–cups of mayo and some hot sauce, to taste. Blend.

LEEK A SECRET

MARCH 18, 2010

Recently I attended a writer's conference at The Kripalu Center for Yoga & Health (kripalu.org). Think holistic hotel, or yoga camp for over-grown kids, and you have the idea: heaven for some, hell for others. Little Miss Rib-Eye, I was somewhat anxious about getting enough protein in this wholesome environment. But after my first meal I was so dazzled by the flavors and the beauty of the food that I didn't want my vegetarian stint to end.

While it's never a bad thing to have others cook for you, reality hits especially hard on a Monday morning trip to the grocery store—what could I buy to recapture some of the magic of the Kripalu weekend? Because I was cooking a meatless dish, I was inspired to buy leeks (which usually I think are a bit too expensive.) Leeks are the secret elite of the onion family, and because they add so much horsepower to a dish I felt the cost would justify my pursuit for perfection. I shopped for freshness, color, and lo-fat flavor and the resulting recipe is truly a Kripalu-worthy dish.

PIGNOLI AND LEEK LINGUINE

Prep: discard the dark green top and bottom tip of 3–leeks. Slice the white and light green parts into thin disks; rinse well in a salad spinner. Toast 1–ounce of Pignoli (pine) nuts. Slice a small head of radicchio into thin ribbons yielding 3–cups. De-stem 6–asparagus spears and cut the veg into 1" pieces. Mince 2–garlic cloves. Measure out 1–cup of white wine; ⅓–cup lemon juice; and 1–cup shaved Parmesan cheese.

Cook 6–ounces of whole-wheat linguine in boiling water for 10 minutes. Before draining, reserve ½–cup of the cooking water.

Heat 1–T of olive oil in a large non-stick pan and sauté leeks on high heat for five minutes. Add garlic and sauté two minutes more. Lower heat; deglaze with a splash of wine. Add asparagus, wine, lemon juice, and cooking water. Simmer for one minute, season with kosher salt and fresh pepper to taste.

Stir in the pasta and half of the Parmesan cheese; turn off the heat and cover. Line two pasta bowls with 1–cup each of the radicchio. Portion out the pasta. Top with generous pinches of gremolata, Pignoli nuts, Parmesan and remaining radicchio Serves 2.

GREMOLATA

In a small processor combine 1–garlic clove; a large handful of clean Italian parsley leaves; and the zest of a small orange. Pulse to mince.

HIP SIPS

APRIL 15, 2010

When it comes to cocktails, James Bond and I are definitely on the same page. In Casino Royale he declares "I never have more than one drink before dinner. But I do like that one to be large and very strong and very cold and very well made. I hate small portions of anything." (007 Martini: 3–shots Gordon's gin, 1–shot vodka, ½-shot of Kina Lillet. Shake 15 seconds, strain into a chilled cocktail glass, twist of lemon, whoop!)

It's time to retire my winter drink (Perfect Manhattan: 2–shots Knob Creek bourbon; ½–ounce, each, red and white vermouth; dash of bitters; shake 15 seconds, strain into a chilled cocktail glass, twist of lemon) in favor of a spring-like celebration libation. I scouted out these cool cocktail recipes currently making the bar rounds. These sips are so good they even make Tax Day seem hip.

ENGLISH ROSE

Cosmos are out—this variation of the classic Martini might be just the thing to sip while you watch your roses bloom. In a shaker filled with ice add 2–shots gin; 1–ounce dry vermouth; 1–ounce apricot brandy; ½–ounce lemon juice; 1–t grenadine. Shake 15 seconds, strain into a chilled cocktail glass, top with a cherry.

GINGER JULEP

A cool Derby variation. In a highball glass muddle a slice of orange; 5–mint leaves; ½–t maple syrup and fresh ginger juice, each. Add 2–shots of Kentucky bourbon and chipped ice, stir.

RASPBERRY MOJITOS

For a chic Cinco de Mayo. In a highball glass, muddle 6–fresh mint leaves; 3–whole raspberries; the juice of one lime; and 2–t of sugar. Add 2–shots of light rum, stir. Fill the glass with chipped ice; top with splash of club soda.

BELLINIS

A Mother's Day delight. Make a peach puree by peeling 4–ripe peaches. Dice and puree in a food processor. Make a raspberry puree by pureeing 1–cup fresh or frozen berries in a food processor. In tall champagne flutes place 1–T of peach puree and 1–t of raspberry puree. Fill glasses with Prosecco.

BURGERS, BREW AND BOCCE

MAY 27, 2010

Time to kick off summer fun by making some memories this holiday weekend. Get the gang together with a simple formula: food, a focus, and fun. My theme is burgers, bocce ball and micro brews. Invite guests to bring a rack of their favorite beer for lots of sampling variety; you provide lemonade, ice tea, and root beer for the crew.

Ask cooking pals to whip up their favorite version of standard salads: potato, coleslaw, greens, and pasta for side dishes. You focus on special burger ideas: salmon burgers with refried beans, avocado, and tomato; beef burgers with blue cheese and bacon; garden burgers with garlic aioli, lettuce, tomato and sweet onion; chicken cutlets with BBQ sauce, Cheddar and pickled red onion; grilled cheese on English muffins for the finicky eaters.

Rolls, ketchup, mustard, mayo, and relish, plus a platter of sliced cheese, pickles, onion, lettuce and tomato are simple essentials. My favorite chips, Kettle Brand Krinkle Cut Potato Chips, serve double duty as hors d'oeuvre and bling for the burgers.

Keep dessert easy and exciting with a self-serve ice cream bar: cones or bowls along with jars of fudge toppings, chopped nuts, cans of whipped cream, and colorful sprinkles.

SALMON BURGERS & REFRIED BEANS

I buy wild salmon burgers in the freezer section of Costco (and some supermarkets); they grill beautifully. The beans take 15 minutes to prep and 45 minutes to simmer; they can be made ahead and freeze well.

Rinse 2–32 ounce cans of kidney beans and add to a large skillet. Stir in 1–large chopped onion; 6–minced cloves of garlic; chopped jalapeno peppers to taste; 2–cups diced carrot; 1–bottle of beer; 3–cups vegetable stock; 1–t Sriracha sauce; 1–ounce of Old El Paso Frajita seasoning mix; and 3–T of chopped preserved lemon (optional, but really good!)

Simmer mixture on med-low, stirring occasionally until most of the liquid has evaporated and the beans are slightly mushy. Smear warm beans over a grilled salmon burger; top with sliced avocado and tomato.

CRANKING THE STANDARD

JUNE 24, 2010

While I love the popular locavore movement ("Is it local? Is it organic? Is it planted by the moon calendar?"), I am noticing a trend of eaters growing crankier about their food in general. Blame it on Starbucks, but our culture has morphed to a dangerous level of food self-consciousness. It feels like oral-cavity overkill: I'm a fat-free, raw foodist, pescatarian, decaf-vegan, macrobiotic, lacto-flexitarian who can't relax at the table. So what. Who wants to cook for these crankavores, anyway?

Even simple baked goods are not safe from the stink eye. I recently served this wonderful Walnut Berry Coffee Cake (vegan, mind you!) and actually had to defend the providence of my cake crumble. Enough already. Here's my standard going forward: "Does it taste good, and, is it a good choice?"

Now that summer and berries are here, there is nothing finer on a sunny morning than chatting with a hot cup of coffee and a delicious pastry. But, if you truly hope to relax, you'll increase the odds by serving up freshly ground/free trade coffee, raw sugar, and local unpasteurized milk (along with organic SPF80.)

WALNUT BERRY COFFEE CAKE

Local strawberries are ripe, so add them to this delightful cake; recipe adapted from *The Kripalu Cookbook* by Atma JoAnn Levitt

Preheat oven to 375°F. In a large bowl, combine 1 ½–cups of whole-wheat pastry flour: 2–cups of white flour: 1–T of baking powder: 1–t baking soda and a pinch of salt.

In a separate bowl, stir together 1–cup water; ⅔–cup rice syrup; ⅓–cup maple syrup; 1–t vanilla and almond extract, each; and ½–cup canola oil. Add the wet ingredients to the dry ingredients and gently blend with a wooden spoon. Pour batter into an oiled 9x12" baking pan; stud the batter with 1–cup chopped local strawberries.

TOPPING

Mix together 1–cup chopped walnuts; ¾–cup ground almonds; ⅔–cup whole-wheat pastry flour; ⅓–cup rice syrup; ⅓–cup maple syrup; and ½–t cinnamon. Loosely spread on top of cake batter. Bake 35–40 minutes.

SWEET SUMMER LUMPIA

JULY 8, 2010

Feeling a little bloated from holiday potluck potato and pasta salads? A recent farmer's market score of bib lettuce, Napa cabbage, scallion, kale, mint, and peas inspired me to create a portable Asian spring roll that is perfect for picnics, parties, or snacks. It's a tasty, healthy way to enjoy the bounty of summer with a little twist.

Variations of Lumpia are common all over Asia. Basically, it's a refreshing no-cook lump of veg and protein that is wrapped in the soft leaves of bib lettuce and doused with a sweet dipping sauce. Ingredients and proportions can be as diverse as the toppings for pizza, so use this recipe as a guideline. But don't eliminate the dry roasted peanuts—they make the dish! Eaten with the hands, Lumpia can be a bit messy, but it is oh-so-delicious summertime fun.

SUMMER LUMPIA WITH SWEET SAUCE

Combine the following in a large prep bowl: 10–sliced scallions; 1–cup diced red pepper; 1–cup diced celery; 8–ounces diced smoked turkey and ham each; 2–cups chopped, pre-cooked shrimp; 1–bunch fresh mint and kale each, ribbon sliced; 12–ounces fresh bean sprouts; and 2–cups fresh or frozen baby peas. Season the batch with a large pinch of kosher salt and red pepper.

Mince 6–garlic cloves and a golf ball-sized chunk of freshly peeled ginger in a mini-processor. Stir half of this paste into the Lumpia; reserve half in the processor.

Slice a head of Napa cabbage into thin ribbons. Place in a large glass bowl and wilt in the micro for 90 seconds, until just barely limp. Drain and combine with Lumpia.

Wash and pat dry 24–bib lettuce leaves of various sizes; place on large serving platter. Add Lumpia to a serving bowl and set on platter. Lightly crush 1–cup of peanuts and place in small side bowl. Fill lettuce leaves with Lumpia, top with Sweet Sauce and peanuts, roll like a cigar, devour.

SWEET SAUCE

To the reserved garlic-ginger paste add 1–cup soy sauce; 2–T of maple syrup or brown sugar; and 2–t of sesame oil, blend well. Serve in a small side bowl.

BOK JOY

SEPTEMBER 23, 2010

I love to grill peaches, bok choy, and shrimp and blanket them with a nutty sauce for the perfect transition-to-autumn meal. This easy Asian dish, loaded with flavor, texture, and eye appeal, features bok choy, a delightful cool weather cabbage now peaking in the fall harvest. Bok choy has a firm white base and dark green leaves; please use baby bok choy—it is the most tender and optimal for this dish.

The peanut sauce is incredible; it has sambal oelek chili paste and peach nectar in it—two cheap, fun ingredients that are in the international section of your supermarket. I first saw this combination of foods in *Bon Appetit* July 2008 issue and I've been enjoying variations on this recipe ever since.

PEANUT SAUCE

Whisk together 6–heaping T of smooth natural peanut butter; ⅓–cup brown sugar; 3–T rice vinegar; 2–T soy sauce; 1–T sambal oelek chili paste; and 5–T peach nectar until smooth; season with kosher salt and pepper to taste.

COCONUT RICE

Oil a deep pot that has a tight fitting lid. Place 2–cups Thai Jasmine rice; 2–cups coconut milk; 1 ¾–cups of water; 2–T shredded unsweetened coconut; pinch of salt together in the pot. On medium-hi heat bring the rice to a gentle bubble, stirring regularly. Turn the heat to lowest setting and cover rice. Simmer 15 minutes. To check for doneness, stir rice with a chopstick. Most of liquid will be absorbed and the rice will be sticky. Turn off heat; rice will stay warm for an hour.

Prep the grill to medium-high heat. Arrange 2–peaches, each cut into 6–wedges; 16–large shrimp on skewers; and 4–heads of Bok choy, halved lengthwise, on the grill. Brush with 4–T of peach nectar. Brush all the items again with ¼–cup of the peanut sauce (use a separate brush for raw shrimp).

Grill until peaches are slightly charred, 2 minutes per side. Grill shrimp and bok choy 3 minutes per side. Mound grilled food onto a platter and drizzle some of the peanut sauce over. Serve sauce and coconut rice on the side. Serves 4.

SECRETS OF THE TUSCAN KITCHEN

OCTOBER 21, 2010

Piano, Piano, Pieno (Slowly, Slowly, Full) is a lovely Italian phrase that captures the essence of Tuscan cuisine. Food that slows us down and fills us up is the stuff of life: a proper meal, at a proper table, with wine, surrounded by loved ones. I recently indulged this delightful routine eating my way through Tuscany—a seductive place of lavender infused hillsides rimmed with olive trees, grapevines, and sunflowers all bathed in extraordinary coffee-colored hues.

I talked to chefs and did a little cooking, too, and learned some "secrets" of the Tuscan kitchen, things we've all known all along, but sometimes forget to practice.

Cibi locali: local, seasonal food. Italians know no other way; there is no locavore fad to embrace, they've lived it forever. What they do with a neighborhood pig is mind-boggling: vast selections of salamis, roasts, and sausages right on down to a simple whipped lardo on toast—it's a gastronomic marvel.

Ore: time to spend, not save. Time to chop tomatoes, zucchini, and porcini mushrooms. Time to mix flour and boil water. Time to read: *The Silver Spoon* is Italy's cooking bible.

Dolci: great desserts. Vin Santo wine, paired with biscotti, is the perfect endnote to a meal; hazelnut studded pan forte with a cappuccino is a must for morning fortification, and several almond ricciarelli cookies complement teatime.

Controni: the essential side dishes. Passion, respect, culture, and love are ingredients that will never be found on a menu or in a cookbook, but they transform our everyday lives piano, piano, pieno.

ALMOND RICCIARELLI COOKIES (REACH-A-RELL-EE)

Preheat oven to 400ºF. Grind up 6–ounces of blanched almonds and pour into a prep bowl. Add 1–cup confectionary sugar; fold in 1–T of flour mixed with ½–t of baking powder. Beat 2–egg whites until stiff and fold into mixture. Add ½–t of almond extract and blend until a soft paste forms.

Place some confectionery sugar on a clean, dry surface. Form 1–T of dough into a small ball; roll in the sugar, then place cookie on a baking sheet covered with parchment. Repeat. Flatten each cookie lightly with a fork. Bake 10–12 minutes until golden. Yields 16 cookies.

MAN UP FOR BRUSSELS SPROUTS

NOVEMBER 4, 2010

Recently I heard some folks talking about Brussels sprouts as though they were some kind of strange bully-vegetable that only brave eaters enjoy. "Brussels sprouts are simply baby cabbages," I said. "If you like salads and coleslaw, then you'll love these yummy morsels, especially if they are prepared well." A couple of guidelines: sprouts must be very fresh; ensure a tender bite by peeling off tough skin; add embellishments you enjoy such as bacon, nuts, butter, herbs and cream. I promise, it will be love at first bite!

BACON-STUDDED BRUSSELS SPROUTS

Plan on 4–7 sprouts per guest depending on the size of the sprouts. Slice off the base and remove tough layers. If Brussels sprouts are larger than a golf ball, then slice each in half and place face down in a large sauté pan (you may need to do two or three batches) add about ⅓–cup of water, cover, and steam for 5 minutes.

Turn up heat, add ⅓–cup of olive oil or good butter, and sauté until the sprouts caramelize a bit; about 5 minutes. Place sprouts in a baking dish; repeat process until you have the desired amount of sprouts. Drizzle maple syrup, sea salt, and red pepper flakes to taste. Toss in cooked chunks of bacon or, better yet, some praline bacon. Shred 1–cup Cheddar cheese over the top and cover with foil. Serve within 20 minutes. If prepping ahead, zap in micro for 3 minutes to reheat.

PRALINE BACON

Preheat oven to 400°F. In a wide, shallow dish combine 1–cup brown sugar; ½–cup roughly ground almonds/pecans; 2–t dry mustard; 1 ½–T of coarse ground pepper; 1–t kosher salt; ⅓–cup mustard seed. Separate 2–pounds of bacon into strips. Dip and press each slice into the sugar mixture on both sides. Lay bacon strips on a large, rimmed baking sheet covered with parchment. Sprinkle excess sugar mixture over the bacon slices in the pan. Roast the bacon until fat begins to render, about 6 minutes. Rotate the pan front–to–back and continue roasting until the bacon is crisp and brown, 8 minutes; cool.

CELEBRATION CAIRO STYLE

DECEMBER 2, 2010

I'm just back from my daughter, Kate's wedding in Cairo. It was quite a party and certainly a new twist on Thanksgiving week! There wasn't a turkey in sight, but we feasted and celebrated Cairo-style. In the Middle East, it is traditional for the groom's family to host the wedding. My darling son-in-law, Fuad, and his lovely family, rolled out the red carpet and treated us to a culinary wonderland of traditional Lebanese and Egyptian foods.

Arab hospitality is convivial and lavish and I routinely submitted to divine excess. My favorites were the nut-and-honey-soaked cakes, Konafa, and the fresh-squeezed mango, guava, and lemon-mint fruit juices that we enjoyed at each meal. Rice dishes are very popular; this is a festive, flavorful one-bowl meal to serve at your own upcoming celebrations. (food photos at kimdannies.com/blog/)

CAIRO CINNAMON RICE

This is a basic oriental-style spiced rice dish that showcases leftovers beautifully. You can add any combination of chicken, beef, shrimp, or lamb; vegetables such as peas, diced carrot, and onion; sultana raisins, dried apricots, dates; rough-chopped blanched almonds, pistachios, and cashews.

For spices, cinnamon and cardamom are traditional and go well with everything, but feel free to vary the flavors according to ingredient choices. For example, add more mint and cumin if you are making a lamb-based rice—have some fun, play with it.

Cook 2–cups of short-grained rice until fluffy. In a large sauté pan melt 3–T of butter; if possible, use samna (the Egyptian name for clarified butter) on medium heat. Add a large pinch of cinnamon and a small pinch of cardamom to the butter and stir lightly. Incorporate the rice by large spoonfuls, coating the rice with the butter; season with salt and pepper until desired flavor is achieved.

Shred some cooked chicken and onions and stir in. Add desired nuts and dried fruit. The rice should be cinnamon colored and very fragrant. Spoon the rice into a serving bowl and pack down firmly. Set for 5 minutes. Optional touch: invert the bowl over a dinner plate so that rice forms a molded shape. Serves 4–8.

2011

CALL ME WILMA

FEBRUARY 2, 2011

I've gone back to the Stone Age, temporarily anyway. I'm eating like a cavewoman in Paleolithic times. Nuts, meats, fruits, leafy greens, eggs, oils, select vegetables. I'm eating this way because my gym-mates (Champlain Valley Crossfit) are doing a forty-five day Paleo challenge. When I learned about the Paleo diet, I protested much about compliance: no dairy, sugar, grains, processed foods, salt, alcohol. When the whine-fest was over, I sucked it up, and jumped in.

Think homemade lemon aioli and pesto sauces; avocados; juicy steaks and lamb chops; chicken and seafood salads loaded with nuts, veggies, and creamy dressing; soups galore; sweet potato rosti; egg salad studded with scallions and bacon. The food is pretty damned good, I must say. And I'm shocked. Never one to follow any kind of diet for longer than 24 hours, I have not missed bread or pasta, cheesy pizza, or dessert. I feel relaxed and coherent, even when ordering lunch at Sky Burger.

The 21st century Paleo diet is pretty simple, there's no calorie counting; when you're full, you stop eating. Choose lean protein, eggs, nuts, seeds, leafy greens and veg (easy on the starchy ones), 3 fruits a day, salt and alcohol in moderation; no dairy, grains, sugar, or processed food. I lost five stubborn pounds in the first two weeks and have yet to suffer hunger pains, or the shame of diet failure. Yabadabado! Kinda liking this cavewoman thing.

PALEO PAD THAI SOUP

In a soup pot, sauté one large chopped onion in a bit of olive oil for 20 minutes. Add 16–ounces of chicken stock and 1–13.5 ounce can organic unsweetened coconut milk. Add 2–cups each of chopped carrot; celery; sweet bell pepper; sliced mushrooms; and cubed raw or cooked chicken. Simmer 15 minutes. Add 5–minced garlic cloves; 2–t curry powder; 1–T freshly minced ginger; and chili seasoning, to taste. Add 2–cups fresh spinach. Serve steaming soup topped with fresh mint, toasted unsweetened coconut, and toasted cashews. Serves 4–6.

PALEO PORCUPINES

For dessert, peel and split a banana in half; slice again length-wise. Drizzle best quality almond butter over the bananas. Roll in toasted sunflower seeds.

SHAM-ROCKED

MARCH 17, 2011

A lover of all things Irish, I always have my eye on the Emerald Isle. Today will not mark a happy St. Patrick's Day there, or any day soon, I fear. Irish eyes are crying as their once flush economy has been flushed down the toilet by banks busting to the tune of ten trillion dollars. The Irish have set a new standard of economic destruction in an era of mind-boggling bank blunders.

With unemployment at 14% the Irish are drinking at home, or leaving home permanently. The local pubs, once the political and cultural heartbeat of a community, are feeling the nasty pinch and closing in record numbers. While one in three beers is still a Guinness, the brand has dropped 8% since December. Despite a 93 billion dollar bailout of the country's banks, this once robust island has been rocked to its core.

For comfort I turn to *The Ballymaloe Cookbook* by Myrtle Allen. Myrtle embodies the essence of stability during times of distress. Her cooking is the most earthy, clean food I have ever had the pleasure of eating. Back in the '70's she single-handedly put Irish cooking on the map, where it thrives today. Maybe Allen's hard-working, passionate style is just what the Irish need to get back to the green.

MYRTLE ALLEN'S BROWN BREAD

Assemble 4–cups whole-wheat flour; 2–packages active dry yeast; 2–cups warm water: 2–T molasses: and 1–T salt.

Put the whole-wheat flour in a large mixing bowl and place in a warm oven. The flour and bowl should be warm when making the bread.

Dissolve yeast in 4–ounces of warm water; blend in the molasses. Let proof. Add another 4–ounces of water. Combine the flour, yeast mixture, and salt. Add enough warm water to create wet, sticky dough. Place in a buttered 9x5x3–inch bread tin. Cover; set in a warm spot. Rise bread to one-third its original size.

Preheat the oven and bake at 450°F for 50 minutes. Remove bread from the pan and leave on the rack of a cooling oven for 20 minutes.

FOND OF FOND

MARCH 31, 2011

"Wow, that was good!" is music to every cook's ears. So what's the secret to making everyday edibles simply incredible? I recently asked myself this question as I watched my buddy, Kiwi Dick, an excellent omelet maker, maneuver in the kitchen. He produced seven perfect omelets with finesse, yet he wasn't confident that he was coaxing the maximum flavor out of his ingredients.

All conscientious cooks aim to create a chain reaction of flavor in their cooking. A mantra worth remembering is "color equals flavor." For sauté, heating the pan until really hot, and then adding the oil is an essential step. When the oil is hot, then it's OK for the ingredients to hit the pan. In the case of onions, the base for almost every savory dish, most cooks need to sauté them quite a bit longer. To achieve maximum intensity of flavor, the onions must release their natural sugars so they can caramelize into gems of glossy brown-black. This goes for mushrooms as well. Incremental pinches of kosher salt throughout the sauté will draw out the water and build seductive layers of flavor.

The hot pan must be scraped continuously; deglazing the onions with a slug of sherry, beer, or stock after 12–15 minutes is where the magic happens.

When onions are allowed to fully caramelize–at around 20 minutes of cooking time–nirvana is within reach. (If you are using garlic, don't add it until the final minute of cooking or it will burn and become bitter.) Scraping of the pan throughout is essential: those shiny, fat-soaked, carbonized treats at the bottom are the "fond." These are the rock stars of flavor that morph a dish from average to amazing.

The culinary cognoscenti agree that the most flavorful cuts of meat are the cheapest—think brisket, pork shoulder, and chuck. Slow, low-heat braising with a bit of decent wine and some root vegetable will yield gravy and a treasure trove of fried black bits tasty enough to start a family fight. So, if it's charred, crunchy, fried, congealed, flecked or globbed, eat it! There's a whole lotta love going on in the fond.

GUILTY, AS CHARGED

APRIL 28, 2011

I confess. I'm a stalker. There is simply no defense for my obsession with the magnificent vegetable, asparagus. When those spring stalks land in my kitchen crosshairs, I cook them into every conceivable dish until even my piggy pugs refuse them.

The simple-sublime way to enjoy asparagus is to start with a big bunch of fat-fingered stalks. Asparagus prep is easy: simply remove the bottom stems by snapping the bases. If the stalks feel a bit tough, peel them gently. Toss the spears in a little olive oil. Fire up the grill and roast the asparagus until they blister and glisten, about 5 minutes. Asparagus is cook-friendly: you can roast it, steam it, sauté it, or zap it in the micro with fine results.

I like to serve a big batch of asparagus on a platter sprinkled with sea salt and fresh pepper. If I have an orange, I'll grate a bit of the zest and then squeeze the juice over the spears. Finely chopped hard-boiled egg looks great, too. There is no better accompaniment to grilled asparagus than a spicy herb aioli.

Chop 6–8 garlic cloves and a bunch of mint leaves in a mini-processor. Add 2–cups of mayo. Season to taste with hot sauce and salt. Blend well. This dish alone will keep me on my best behavior—at least until strawberry-stalker season begins.

ORECCHIETTE SPRING FLING

Boil water to cook a pound of orecchiette pasta. Chop a large onion. Heat a large pan. Add 1–T of olive oil. Sauté the onions 15 minutes; stir often. Prep and cut 2–pounds of asparagus stalks into thirds. Add to the sauté along with 1–T of olive oil; and 3–chopped garlic cloves. Sauté for 5 minutes more, stirring often.

Drain pasta, reserving ½–cup of the cooking water. Add the pasta water to the sauté pan along with a 1–cup of ricotta or crème fraiche. Stir well. Fold in pasta. Blend well, season to taste. Cover and heat through for 5 minutes. To serve, top with freshly grated Parmesan cheese and chopped fresh chives. Serves 4.

SUMMER'S SWEET SPOT

JULY 7, 2011

We are in the cooking sweet spot, where that special kind of satisfaction that cooking outside on a hot summer night affords. Now that we are on high BBQ alert, it's time to freshen up the traditional accompaniment to sauce slathered meat: coleslaw.

I like to start with a variety of cabbage heads such as Chinese, Savoy, and Napa; they taste far fresher than pre-packaged green cabbage and the variety of textures guarantees a lively salad. Add colorful radicchio, shredded carrot, tart green apple, crunchy ramen noodles, and slivered almonds, and you've got a party on a platter. Which reminds me. Try mixing the salad and dressing just before mealtime and plating the coleslaw on a large platter—it is stunning, and will take a drippy basic to a new level of culinary sophistication.

COLESLAW WITH A TWIST

Choose small heads of Chinese, Napa, Savoy cabbage, and Radicchio. Peel off outer layer and discard. Slice each head in half and remove tough core. Thinly slice each half-moon cabbage into ribbon–thin cuts. Combine cabbage in a large prep bowl. Shred 2–3 large carrots and add to the mix. (Prep one day ahead; seal in zip-lock bags).

Cut 1–2 green apples into a small dice and toss with the mix. Toast 4–6 ounces of slivered almonds. Crumble 1–2 packages of ramen noodles. Just before serving, add the desired amounts of apple, nuts, and ramen. Using tongs, fold in a cup of the dressing. Judge how much dressing you like, conservatively adding as you go.

Turn coleslaw onto a large serving platter and sprinkle with fresh chive or mint. Serves 10–20, depending on prep amounts.

CREAMY GINGER DRESSING

This is a fun semi-homemade dressing. In a small processor chop 2–garlic cloves and 3 quarter-sized disks of fresh ginger. Add the zest of one lemon and mince. Add 1–8 ounce jar of Marie's Coleslaw dressing. Add ½–cup of lemon juice. Mix well and adjust for taste with salt and pepper. If you have poppy, celery, or mustard seeds, toss in a generous pinch.

HOT FUN IN THE SUMMER TIME

AUGUST 18, 2011

Tired of slaving over a hot grill while the gang chats and sucks on gin and tonics? I am. For the rest of the summer I'm prepping ahead and staying cool. That means simple salads, pre-grilled proteins, and fun pasta swimming in a pool of fresh tomato and basil. This is the perfect time of year to break out those exotic jars of sauces lurking in your pantry. Pair them with shrimp and chicken kabobs, both excellent candidates for the grill/chill prep plan. Put out wraps or pita, tomatoes and fresh greens, and you've got a cool meal and some hot fun.

TORTELLINI CAPRESE

Cook 2–9 ounce packages of fresh tortellini; drain to a prep bowl. Rough dice 3–tomatoes, removing seeds; add to bowl. Ribbon-cut lots of fresh basil; add to bowl. Cube 3–ounces of fresh mozzarella, add. In a small processor mince the zest of one orange. Add 3–garlic cloves, mince. Add the juice from the orange plus 2–T of bottled orange juice, and ⅓–cup olive oil. Blend well. Fold dressing over the pasta. Season with sea salt and freshly ground pepper. Prep up to 24 hours ahead; serves 4–8.

PROSCIUTTO DI PARMA GREENS

8 hour do ahead: cube-cut 2 ripe/firm avocados, place in a small bowl along with one avocado nut and douse lightly with lemon juice. Remove the seeds and rough dice 4 tomatoes. Place in a small bowl and sprinkle with kosher salt. Cover both bowls and rest at room temperature. Clean fresh field greens, measuring out a generous handful per portion. Chill greens in a plastic bag. Add 1–garlic clove to a small jar. Add ¼–cup lemon juice, 1–T Dijon mustard, ½–cup olive oil, a pinch of salt and pepper. Seal.

Assemble salad: Shake dressing well and add desired amount to the greens. Toss gently until lightly coated. Pile greens on a large rectangular platter. Using best quality Prosciutto place small mounds of meat along border of the platter, forming casual "rosettes." Scatter tomato and avocado down the salad's spine. Season with sea salt and freshly ground pepper.

AND THE BEET GOES ON

SEPTEMBER 15, 2011

As you read this column I'll be trudging my way to the summit of Mt. Rainier. It won't be a sprint and it won't be a death march—just a slow, roped-in, steady beat strapped with a forty-pound pack. The things we do for love. I won't be eating well, either. The grub is the stuff of my nightmares: beef jerky, granola bars, powdered mysteries.

Instead, I'll be fantasizing about delicious food, most probably beets. I am besotted with beets. And I'll be dreaming of my cozy kitchen and cooking up a welcome home feast. It's time to turn a season, presenting old favorites in a new fashion worthy of a reunion dinner. I'll roast local leg of lamb and splurge on Vermont Creamery goat cheese, bake a beautiful beet gratin, and uncork a Big Barn Red. With a song in my heart, you can be sure I'll be celebrating moonlight in Vermont.

VERMONT BEET & APPLE GRATIN

Preheat oven to 375°F. Peel and halve 3–pounds of beets; steam for 20 minutes; drain and cool. Cut into a medium dice; drizzle with ¼–cup apple cider vinegar. Reserve.

Core 3–golden delicious apples, but don't peel. Cut into a medium dice. Melt 2–ounces of butter in a large skillet and sauté the apples, stirring often, over medium-high heat for 2 minutes. Add ½-cup of fresh apple cider, cooking 3 minutes longer. Remove from heat; add beets.

In a prep bowl combine 1–cup light cream; 1–T salt; 1–t, each, pepper and nutmeg; 3–T fresh horseradish; 2–T freshly chopped sage. Stir well. Grease a casserole dish with butter. Add the beets and apples. Crumble 4–ounces of goat cheese over the beets. Pour the cream all over the beets. Cover and bake the gratin for 20 minutes. Remove foil and top the casserole with 3–cups of breadcrumbs that have been cut with 2–ounces of butter. Bake 20–30 minutes more until golden brown. Serves 8–10; reheats well.

GLEANING THE GARDEN

SEPTEMBER 29, 2011

I push back the ache of summer's end by rooting around in the garden. Seeds are scattered for next year's blossoms and remaining herbs are snipped to create compound butters. My green-thumbed neighbor delivers a rocket-sized zucchini, a bittersweet gift I am grateful for; nothing goes to waste. Like summer memories, the precious dregs of Vermont's abbreviated harvest are bound for the freezer to be savored in deep winter.

Giant vegetables mandate that the soup season begin in earnest. I'm lucky to have grown up with the Soup Goddess. My mom is more than a little celebrated for her heavenly concoctions served up each Monday at Williston's Vermont Respite House. Although she never works from a recipe, mom has graciously documented her zucchini soup. She'll tell you that instinct, love, and lots of practice are the essentials for a great soup. I'd say that goes double for gardening and motherhood.

PAT MYETTE'S ZUCCHINI TOMATO SOUP

In a large pot combine 2–overgrown unpeeled zucchini, cut and seeded into medium chunks, with 1–quart of chicken stock. Simmer until the zucchini softens, 20 minutes. Reserve.

In a large soup pot heat 1–T canola oil and 1–T butter. Add 2–cups of diced onion;

1–cup diced celery; and 2–cups diced carrots. Cover and simmer 10 minutes over medium heat until tender. Add 3–T of tomato paste, stir well, and cook 2 minutes longer.

Add reserved zucchini and stock to the pot. Simmer 25 minutes on medium heat. Cool slightly. To puree mixture, use a stick blender right in the pot. If you don't have one, transfer soup to a food blender and puree to desired texture. Season with salt and pepper, to taste. To serve, top with freshly chopped chives (optional). Serves 8.

COMPOUND BUTTER

Mix best quality butter with any combination of chopped herbs, garlic, lemon and orange zest, olives, capers, or Parmesan cheese. Roll butter into golf ball sized rounds and wrap tightly in plastic. Freeze individually, and then store the like-flavored balls in labeled quart sized Ziploc bags. Use the butter to flavor soups, stews, and crostini.

FANCY FRENCH PIE

OCTOBER 27, 2011

An extra-special occasion dessert is Apple Tarte Tatin, a succulent upside-down apple pie. Officially known as La Tarte Desmoiselles Tatin, this classic is named for the French sisters who created it in 1898. This was my favorite recipe that I learned at La Varenne in 1995. I bought the gorgeous copper 12" pan that I make it in at the famous E. Dehillerin cook shop in Paris. In fact, I hand-carried two of them on the plane—one for myself, and one for my gourmet mom.

Apple Tarte Tatin is extraordinary due to the intensity of flavor from the caramelized sugar, apples, and butter. A fundamental of French pastry cooking is "color equals flavor" so don't be alarmed if your caramel topping is quite dark—that is considered très bien!

PÂTE BRISÉE (PASTRY CRUST)

In a food processor combine 4–cups white pastry flour; 2–T sugar; and 1–cup chilled butter cut into small chunks. Pulse quickly until coarse flour forms. With the motor running, add one-half cup cold water and let the dough form. Add small drops as needed to incorporate all of the flour. The dough must pull cleanly off the sides of the working bowl. Remove the pastry and wrap in plastic wrap, store in the fridge.

TARTE TATIN (APPLE TART)

Peel and core 12–14 golden delicious apples; slice a thin layer off each bottom to even the base, and then slice each apple in half. Preheat oven to 400°F. On the stovetop, in a large

(12–14" wide) cast iron pan or deep copper tart pan, melt 1–cup butter with 2–cups sugar. Turn off heat. In a concentric circle arrange the apples standing them tightly against each other, back-to-belly style, until the pan is filled.

Caramelize the apples on medium heat for about 30 minutes or until a dark syrup bubbles up and you can smell the cooked sugar. Let the apples cool slightly, then roll out the pastry and fit on top of the apples, working quickly and tucking in the edges.

Bake for 20–30 minutes, until pastry is golden brown. Cool tart 10 minutes; gently unmold tart onto a round serving platter. Don't panic if the entire apple does not release! Simply use a spatula to re-paste the apples, scraping up as much color as possible. As the tart cools it will solidify to perfection. You can make this two days ahead; cool tart, then wrap in plastic and then foil. Serve slices with a dollop of crème fraîche; serves 14–16.

READY, SET, PARTY!

NOVEMBER 10, 2011

Before you know it hungry holiday guests will be flowing through the door, so divert kitchen drama by planning ahead. I love classic recipes, and this Chicken Marbella is a spectacular party dish that feeds an army cheaply. The recipe is from the 1979 *Silver Palate*, the seminal cookbook that inspired my generation of cooks with practical and appealing food.

According to the authors, Rosso & Lukins, "the overnight marinating of the chicken is essential to the moistness of the finished product; the chicken keeps well and even improves over several days..." To me, that shouts, "Do ahead recipe!" my favorite strategy for welcoming guests. Marbella is Spanish-influenced, so crusty bread and a lusty Rioja wine are a great match for this party meal.

CHICKEN MARBELLA

Quarter 4–chickens (2 ½–pounds each). Place in a large bowl. In a medium-sized bowl combine ¼–cup dried oregano; 2–large pinches of kosher salt and pepper; ½–cup red wine vinegar; ½–cup olive oil. Peel and puree a head of garlic. Add garlic puree to the mix and stir well.

Now, add 1–cup pitted prunes; 1–cup pitted Spanish green olives; ½–cup capers with a bit of juice; and 6–bay leaves. Stir well and pour the marinade over the chicken. Cover and marinate overnight (or longer) in fridge.

To serve: preheat oven to 375°F. Arrange chicken in a single layer in one or two large, shallow baking pans. Spoon the marinade evenly over the chicken. Sprinkle the chicken with 1–cup brown sugar and pour 1–cup white wine or sherry among the batch. Bake 60 minutes, basting frequently with pan juices.

Choose a large serving platter. If desired, whip up a batch of fluffy couscous—it makes a useful "bed" for the serving platter. With a slotted spoon transfer chicken, prunes, olives, and capers to the platter. Moisten the chicken with a few tablespoons of the pan juices and garnish with freshly chopped parsley. Pour the remaining pan juices into a sauceboat and serve on the side. Serves 10–12.

A SEASONAL STUNNER

DECEMBER 22, 2011

Looking for a last minute showstopper for your holiday dinner? Or how about something special to ring in the New Year? Either way you'll be set with this quick and gorgeous Roasted Pork with Dried Fruit & Port Sauce. My neighbor and fabulous cook, JanaG, turned me on to this meal courtesy of *Southern Living* magazine (November 2010). This recipe is adapted from the original.

ROASTED PORK & FRUIT SAUCE

In a glass bowl combine ½–cup, each, of dried fruit: apricots, prunes, blueberries and cherries. Pour 1–cup of apple cider over, cover with plastic wrap and zap for 1 minute on hi in microwave. Let mixture sit at room temperature; you can prep this 30 minutes (and up to 24 hours) ahead.

Preheat oven to 425°F. Sprinkle 3–pounds of pork tenderloin with salt and pepper. Heat 2–T of oil in a large skillet and sear the pork for three minutes on two sides or until golden brown. Place pork in a roasting pan; reserve drippings in the skillet. Roast pork at 425°F for 18–20 minutes, or until a meat thermometer inserted into the thickest portion registers 150°F. Remove from oven, cover and let stand 10 minutes.

To the hot skillet add ½–cup pine nuts. Sauté the nuts for 2 minutes on medium heat, until the nuts are fragrant. Add 1–cup port wine or drinking sherry (NOT supermarket cooking sherry!); ½–cup apple cider; 2–minced garlic cloves; and a pinch of cinnamon and salt. Bring to a boil; reduce heat to low, add reserved fruit and simmer 5 minutes or until mixture thickens slightly.

Stir in ½–cup of chicken broth and simmer the sauce for 15 minutes, or until the fruit is tender and plump and the sauce is glossy and slightly syrupy. To serve, slice pork and place on a warm serving platter, top with some of the fruit and sauce; serve remainder of sauce in a side dish. Serves 6.

2012

SOLIDLY SENTI-MENTAL

JANUARY 12, 2012

"When I walk into my kitchen today, I am not alone. Whether we know it or not, none of us is. We bring fathers and mothers and kitchen tables, and every meal we have ever eaten. Food is never just food. It's also a way at getting at something else: who we are, who we have been, and who we want to be."

—Molly Wizenberg from *A Homemade Life*

In a post-holiday reflective mood I waded through piles of clippings, recipes and food photos that have caught my eye over the years. I found this poem, which I love, and some recipes that my mom and I created together thirty years ago that still appeal. As I examined my youthful script on 5x8" recipe cards coated with plastic, I smiled recalling those moments of discovery at the kitchen table, writing out our masterpieces as I fell solidly head-over-heals in love with cooking.

Our all–time favorite, a do-ahead red pepper puree recipe is easy, healthy, versatile and gorgeous to look at; it's a superb staple for the fridge. I use it like mayo for topping vegetables, shrimp pasta, infusing soups, and drizzling over tacos. You can change the vibrant color by substituting sweet yellow or orange peppers. For a spicier version, add more pepper flakes.

HARICOT VERT & RED PEPPER PUREE

Chop 6–large sweet peppers (remove ribs and seeds). In a large non-stick sauté pan heat 3–T of olive oil or butter. Add the peppers along with a large pinch of salt; 2–T of sugar; 2–T white vinegar; 1–t sweet paprika; and ¼–t of dried red pepper flakes. Cover and simmer 45 minutes until peppers are very soft.

Uncover pan, increase heat to medium and stir until the liquid evaporates. Allow peppers to rest for ten minutes. Pour the batch into a food processor and pulse until a smooth puree forms. Taste and adjust for seasoning. Makes 3–cups; stores well in the fridge for 10 days.

Haricot Vert–the thin French baby green beans–are prettiest in this recipe (Costco has a steady supply), but any fresh green bean will work. Simply steam a bundle of beans in 1–cup of water in a large covered sauté pan for 6–8 minutes. Drain and plate. Nap the pepper puree over the beans and top with a handful of toasted pecans and crumbled goat cheese (optional).

KISS A FROG

JANUARY 26, 2012

Often called celery root, celeriac will never be confused with its pretty cousin, true celery. So what if this bulbous dome, dotted by dangling hairy rootlets and dirt-filled crevices is the geek-boy at the dance? A quick shower and shave with a sharp peeler will soon reveal its princely flesh.

Celeriac delivers character and a bracing clean flavor: a cross between parsley and celery, only deeper, softer, and slightly sweet. Shred it, roast it, puree it—celeriac adds a creamy volume, nutrition, and flavor to dishes while remaining discreet. We're talkin' marriage material here, people.

When the word gets out, celeriac will be winter's hit veg, showing up at parties everywhere. Eaters will wonder aloud why a particular dish of yours is so outrageously delicious. Go ahead, enjoy a quiet affair with this understated hero, you won't regret it.

CELERIAC SALAD WITH AIOLI

Peel one large knob of celery root, rinse. Shred raw root in a food processor or grate by hand. You'll be rewarded with mounds of snow white, crunchy slaw. Place in a prep bowl.

Aioli: in a small processor, finely mince 3–4 garlic cloves. Add 1–heaping T of Dijon mustard; the juice of a lemon; 1–cup of Hellmann's mayo; 1–T tomato paste; and a pinch of red pepper flakes. Process 30 seconds. Adjust seasoning with kosher salt. Fold the aioli over the celery root. Top with several handfuls of clean flat-leaf parsley. Serve immediately, or store in fridge up to one day ahead; serves 4–6.

CREAMY POTATO & CELERIAC SOUP

Peel 6–medium red potatoes and cut into quarters. Peel one celeriac root and shred. Place all the veg in a cooking pot and cover with vegetable or chicken stock. Add 6–whole garlic cloves and 1–medium chopped onion. Cover and bring to a full boil on high heat, then simmer the soup for 20 minutes until potatoes are very soft.

Warm 1 ½–cups of low fat milk with 2–T of sherry and 2–T of butter in the microwave, on hi, for 1 minute. Mash the potatoes and add the milk mixture. Puree the soup until it is smooth. Adjust flavor with kosher salt and pepper. Serves 6–8.

KITCHEN MIRTH

MARCH 22, 2012

Certain vegetables have reputations for being very naughty girls, when, in fact, they're only guilty of consorting with the wrong kind of (cooking) crowd. Case in point: eggplant, the Lily Bart of the food world. While raised to be a good and proper vegetable, gossipmongers perpetuate the notion that she's a leech, or even worse, a full-blown oil sucker. These rumors have taken root only because cooks have consistently mistreated her. They blindly follow traditional recipes that call for one to two cups of olive oil as a standard way of preparation. It's turned eggplant into a social pariah, a calorie-loaded burden that no one wants to be seen with.

Another vicious rumor about elegant eggplant is that she's fussy, that she needs to sit salted for hours before cooking, or she will behave bitterly. This is simply not true. Eggplant is sweet and well mannered and full of character. Buy a mid-sized firm-fleshed beauty, cook it sooner than later, and you will have no problem with the lady.

It's time society stood up for beautiful, healthful, delicious eggplant. The simple truth is that one good sized eggplant can be coated in 1–2 T of oil (via a gallon Ziploc bag) and she will comport herself just as well as one soaked in cups of hot oil. Eggplant thrives on being invited to dine: roast, stew, even fry her, but please—kindly quit maligning her.

SEARED TUNA & EGGPLANT

Peel and cube a medium sized eggplant and toss with 1–2 T of olive oil. In a hot non-stick sauté pan add 1–medium chopped onion and 2–sliced celery stalks; sauté for 10 minutes, drizzling in a small amount of oil if needed. Add the eggplant and sear, turning, for 2 minutes. Add 2–cups of crushed tomato; 3–minced garlic cloves; 1–T capers; 3–T chopped olives; 3–minced anchovies; and salt and pepper to taste. Stir in 1–T red wine vinegar and 1–t sugar. Simmer covered for 15 minutes. Grill tuna steaks to desired temperature, top with plenty of the sauce. Serves 6.

THE HUNGER GAMES

APRIL 19, 2012

Time for a spring tune-up in the pantry and the pants. Here are some food-savvy tips to incorporate into your eating game plan. While strategies abound for fitness and food regimes, there is only one winner in the hunger games, and that's *YOU* (when exercise meets healthy food choices on a daily basis.) Sure, you've heard it all before, but a spring refresher can't hurt. And I think you'll love my Fudgie Babies—they are to die for.

Lose the bite and gain the flavor of healthy cancer-fighting onions in your dishes. Rinsing minced onions in cool water removes the pungency that can overpower other flavors. When onions are chopped, sulfurous compounds are released as the knife slices through cell walls. Washing the sulfur from the cell walls results in a mellow, aromatic flavor.

Cooking healthy is easy with a "less is more" approach. Chose foods in their natural state, cook with olive oil, and add a small amount of sea salt to finish. *Do no harm*, which means, sear, grill, or sauté foods quickly to retain flavors. Stick with fresh fruits, and vegetables, whole grains, and clean proteins. Eschew processed foods.

When ordering out split an entree with someone (or divide and pack half for another meal) as a matter of routine. This really works!

Most recipes call for too much oil or butter; you can generally cut back to half of the recipe recommendation. Also, coconut oil cooking spray for lightly coating meats and veggies is a healthy trick.

Stuck in the car and dying of hunger? Keep a few "Think Thin" bars in your glove compartment for emergencies. These tasty, high-protein bars are the cleanest, yummiest lifesaver you'll find in a supermarket.

FUDGIE BABIES

In a food processor crush ½–cup of salted almonds; remove, reserve.

To the processor add ½–cup of walnuts and crush. Add 1 ½–cups of date pulp; 4–T of cocoa powder; 1–t of vanilla; and a pinch of salt and cinnamon. Pulse to combine. Divide dough into two sections; roll dough on pieces of plastic wrap into a plump log shape. Coat the logs with almonds. Seal in wrap and freeze 2 hours. Slice and serve.

BUN BATHING

JULY 12, 2012

Pan Bagnat (phan bahn-YAH), or bathed bread, is a Niçoise salad inspired sandwich that shouts "summer!" Pressed between two rounds of artisan bread you'll find tuna, egg, black olive, caper, tomato, roasted red pepper, arugula, and a mustard-anchovy infused vinaigrette. The concoction is wrapped tightly in plastic and refrigerated overnight so that the spunky dressing bathes the bread, soaking in flavor and moisture. It is the perfect picnic sandwich; a 16–ounce round of bread will feed six hungry friends. I like to use Red Hen Bakery's Cyrus Pringle loaf.

Julia Child introduced Americans to this French Riviera classic warning that "the oil from the dressing should run down your arm when you eat Pan Bagnat." I don't recommend this as a sunscreen strategy, but I can't think of anything more deliciously sensuous than devouring this feast, fresh from a swim on a hot July afternoon, arms dripping oily dressing and hands clasping icy beers.

PAN BAGNAT

Vinaigrette: in a small jar with a cover combine 4–T virgin olive oil, the juice of a lemon; 2–t Dijon mustard; 1 or 2–T anchovy paste; 1–T minced shallot; 2–minced garlic cloves; fresh pepper and sea salt to taste. Shake well to emulsify, adjust for seasoning. The dressing will be robust in flavor.

Next, hard-boil two eggs; cool and slice. Roast a sweet red pepper over the open flame on a gas stove (or use ½–cup bottled red peppers, dried on paper towel). Chop ⅓–cup pitted kalamata olives and combine with 1–T capers. Slice 2–3 tomatoes (enough to cover bread surface.) Drain and flake 2 6–ounce cans of tuna packed in oil.

Compose the Pan Bagnat: slice a round 16–ounce bread in half through the middle. Bathe the surface of each half with the vinaigrette. Cover each surface with fresh arugula leaves. Layer the remaining ingredients onto bottom half of the bread and cap with the top half. Wrap tightly in several layers of plastic wrap. Place Pan Bagnat in fridge with a heavy weight to compress it; set overnight, or at least three hours.

SIMPLE SUMMER SWEETS

JULY 26, 2012

This is your moment to let summer's bounty of gorgeous ingredients do the work while you take the bows (or lie in the hammock with a gin & tonic). Red ripe tomatoes studded with sea salt; grilled zucchini, eggplant and onions glistening in olive oil and rosemary; local salad greens; cold cubed watermelon—easy food that's fast to the table and kind to the waistline. This leaves plenty of room to enjoy a quotidian summer sweet. A bite of fresh berry crumble or lemon tart is the essence of summer in every spoonful.

BLARNEY COTTAGE CRUMBLE

My mom whipped up this gem up at the lake last week—it is so yummy!

Preheat oven to 350°F. In an 8" glass pie plate combine 3–chopped PA peaches; 1–cup blueberries; 12–pitted cherries; 1–t cornstarch; 2–T sugar; and the zest of one lemon. Melt 2–T of butter and combine with 1–cup commercial granola mix, 1–T flour and a pinch of cinnamon. Sprinkle granola mixture over the fruit. Bake 25 minutes or until it bubbles. Top with vanilla ice cream.

ALMOND TART CRUST

Preheat oven to 350°F. Spray 9" tart pan with non-stick spray. In a food processor combine 1–cup flour; ½–cup sliced almonds; ¼–cup sugar; and ¼–t kosher salt. Add 6–T of unsalted butter, cubed and cold; add 1–t almond extract, then pulse to blend. Dribble in 3–5 T of ice water until dough forms. Pack dough into a sheet of plastic wrap and chill 30 minutes. Preheat oven to 425°F. Roll out dough, place in pan, trim, and freeze for 20 minutes. Bake 20–25 minutes.

PUCKER-UP LEMON CURD

Whisk together in a sauce pan: 3–whole eggs; 3 egg yolks; 1–cup sugar; ¾–cup fresh lemon juice; 2–T lemon zest; a pinch of salt; 6–T unsalted butter, cubed. Cook over medium heat, whisking constantly until filling thickens slightly, about 5 minutes. Pour into pre-baked crust and bake at 325°F for 10 minutes. Cool tart for 30 minutes. Load up the cooled tart with fresh berries and peaches; top with whipped cream or mascarpone.

PRETTY YUM FUN

AUGUST 9, 2012

Each day I want to be aware of a beautiful moment, a delicious moment, and a funny moment. Now, I don't know what might be funny about tomatoes, except some of their names ('Limmony', 'Mortgage Lifter', 'Mr. Stripey'), but I do know they provide a riot of beautiful color and a delicious moment each and every day of August. Is there anything more gorgeous or mouthwatering than a thick slice of tangerine orange tomato glistening with sea salt?

We are in the 'less is more' season where just a few fantastic peak ingredients can nicely satisfy our desire for beauty and sustenance. All a cook needs for this month's menu is local produce and the following: a box of Maldon sea salt, a pepper mill, fresh garlic and herbs, olive oil, lemons, olives, nuts, local cheeses like feta, burrata, or goat, and a big white serving platter. Add whatever protein you fancy, and you have magic in the making.

OLYMPIC PROVISIONS CAPRESE

A family favorite is Caprese Salad (tomato, basil, and fresh mozzarella.) After several rounds of it some variation is in order. This recipe combines eye candy and a whole new flavor platform for your palate. I had this salad at Olympic Provisions in the marvelous food town of Portland, Oregon.

Salad portions are per person, so multiply amounts: 1–sliced local tomato; 2–ounces of crumbled goat cheese; a handful of local greens, ½–cup of melon cubes;

6–slices of cucumber, halved; and big pinches of fresh mint and basil leaves.

On a large serving platter arrange the greens, tomatoes and herbs. Scatter the melon and cucumbers and goat cheese. Drizzle desired amount of Lemon Basil Dressing over the salad and top with a grind of fresh pepper.

LEMON BASIL DRESSING

In a mini chopper mince 1–garlic clove. Add a handful of basil and mint leaves and pulse to mince. Add ¼–cup of fresh lemon juice and ¾–cup of best quality olive oil, a generous pinch of sea salt and fresh pepper. Blend well. Yields 1–cup.

FRITTER FRISSON

AUGUST 23, 2012

Who knew leftover corn could be sexy? Those uneaten cobs, sitting like abandoned corpses on your counter, can easily be transformed into crispy, hot, sweet corn fritters. This is fun, fast, 'eat with your hands' food that requires no practice, and will WOW your crowd in less than twenty minutes.

Don't be shy about fritter—this recipe uses very little oil and it won't make your kitchen smell like a rancid take-out joint. I'd go so far as to call it a healthy treat. Fritter batter is a lot like making pizza, there are a hundred ways to do it, it all tastes good, and you really cannot blow it. I made my recipe ridiculously easy to remember, so that going forward fritters are never a chore. The Maple Chipotle Sauce is so alluring and addictive it could double as a dab behind the ears.

More good news: make the fritter batter 36-hours ahead and chill. This allows you to whip up small batches when desire strikes. It's time to reignite the flame of passion for leftover local corn via golden, crunchy fritters—the produce section will be boring soon enough.

CRISPY CORN FRITTERS

Combine 1–cup milk; 1–egg; and 1–T soft butter. Mix ½–cup flour; ½–cup corn meal; ¼–t each of baking powder, curry, salt, and red pepper flakes. Add 3–cups shucked corn (raw or cooked); 3–slices of cooked, chopped bacon; and 3–T freshly chopped chives.

Heat a large non-stick frying pan; add ¼–cup coconut oil. When the oil is hot, spoon 1–T of batter for each fritter into the pan spacing a half-inch apart. Cook over medium-high heat for 1–2 minutes, until golden brown underneath, then turn and cook the other side for 2 minutes. Transfer to a cookie sheet lined with paper towels. Sprinkle with sea salt; keep warm in 200ºF oven. Repeat with remaining batter, adding more oil. Yield: 32 fritters.

MAPLE CHIPOTLE SAUCE

In a prep bowl combine 1 ½–cups of mayo with 2–T each maple syrup and supermarket brand chipotle sauce. Adjust for seasoning with pinches of salt.

TOAST THE SCHOOL YEAR

SEPTEMBER 20, 2012

Now that our summer groove has ground to a halt, it's time to pull out a few tricks to keep the gang moving forward with the school routine. It's called 'breakfast for dinner' a loving and revered tradition among desperate moms. Baked Blueberry French Toast is just the right amount of wrong on a busy school night. It's a fun treat for kids to make and eat, and it will morph a feeble C-minus dinner effort to the honor roll. Just make sure to serve a big mint-studded fresh fruit salad along side to keep you out of the Principal's office.

BAKED BLUEBERRY FRENCH TOAST

Spray a 9x12" baking dish with cooking oil spray. Line the pan with 6–supermarket sesame steak rolls. Mix together 6–eggs with ½–cup of milk. Add small pinches of cinnamon, ginger, and salt. Pour over the rolls and set 15 minutes or even overnight. Bake, uncovered, in a preheated 425°F oven for 15 minutes, then add Crumble Topping and bake for 15 minutes more. Serve with Blueberry Maple Syrup; serves 4.

Crumble Topping: combine ½–cup cold butter bits; ¾–cup of flour; ⅓–cup brown sugar; and ½–cup of crushed walnuts.

BLUEBERRY MAPLE SYRUP

In a glass container combine 1–cup of Vermont maple syrup with 1–cup fresh or frozen blueberries. Cover with plastic wrap. Zap in microwave for 2 minutes.

Pump the Nutrition: A nice alternative is to add pizza fillings such as cheese, sausage, and spinach to the inside of the rolls and proceed with egg mixture, leaving out the spices and crumble topping, for a calzone-style baked toast. To serve, top with warm marinara sauce.

FRESH FRUIT SALAD

Your family will eat more fruit if it is cut up. Kids love toothpicks, so stud your salad with picks and let them have at it. Start with a ripe cantaloupe melon. Cut it in half and scoop out the seeds. Slice into wedges, then slide a knife along the base of each wedge to release it from the rind. Chop into chunks. Add to a serving bowl along with store-prepped pineapple, green grapes, and raspberries. Top with freshly chopped mint.

STOMACH TRUMPS STUBBORN

OCTOBER 14, 2012

The happiest of cooks don't necessarily have the finest cooking skills or the most knowledge, they just happen to make the most of every eating opportunity that comes their way. My husband loves to eat—you will find no finer appetite among men, yet he rarely lifts a saucepan. Despite thirty years of gentle cajoling, raucous cheerleading, and overt threats, he simply does not choose to cook.

It finally came to pass that I was away a few weeks ago, and he was going to have to step up to the proverbial plate, as it were, if we were to enjoy any kind of decent reunion meal. Stomach trumps stubborn! Together we came up with this menu, and it was mind-blowingly good. He was floored at how easy it is to produce a restaurant-quality meal with very little knowledge and even less effort. Lesson learned: if you want to encourage a reluctant cook, be sure to sandwich every slice of mandate between two juicy layers of easy execution and praise.

JEFF'S CROCK POT SHORT RIBS

Wide, shallow pasta bowls make for an especially attractive presentation.

In a crockpot combine 1–cup chopped onion; 2–cups red wine; and 1–cup BBQ sauce. Add 4–pounds of boneless beef short ribs. Coat the beef with the sauce and turn the crockpot on to low for 6 hours.

Twenty minutes before dinner, remove the meat and tent in foil. In a saucepan, boil the crockpot liquid until the volume is reduced by half. Pour into a measuring cup and drain off fat. Taste and adjust for seasoning. If it is too salty, add a touch of maple syrup. If it is too bland, a pinch of salt or spritz of vinegar will do the trick.

Boil 1–cup of Italian couscous (fat, pearl-like pasta) in 4–cups of water, for 8 minutes. Drain and reserve. Slice 1–carrot and 1–zucchini into 2" batons and sauté 8 minutes in 1–T butter; season with salt and pepper.

To serve, place a scoop of couscous into each pasta bowl. Pour some of the heated sauce over the couscous. Pile on the rib meat and arrange the vegetables. Serves 2 hungry people.

MEAL CULPA

OCTOBER 18, 2012

i'm sorry for
what i said
when i was hungry

A friend sent me this. It's kitschy and it made me realize why fuses DO seem shorter and the line between mere decorum and actual aggression grows blurrier as the autumn days grow darker. Triggering the state of "hangry" creates ugly consequences for us and for the innocent victims in our immediate vicinity. It's the food equivalent of Flip Wilson's '*the devil made me do it.*'

When the body starts to feel hungry (the Brits call it "peckish") levels of the brain chemical serotonin dip, erupting rabid emotions like anxiety and crabbiness. These fluctuating serotonin levels affect the brain regions that enable us to regulate anger, making us prone to aggression when hungry. The onset of dark winter days compounds this problem.

Williston's own Dr. Deb Norton says that "Not satisfying hunger, for example, when you are dieting or simply don't have time to eat can cause low blood sugar or clinical hypoglycemia. This happens to a varying degree amongst those of us who do not have diabetes (folks with diabetes can have profound hypoglycemia that can lead to dangerous circumstances). The brain is one of the vital organs that is deprived of sugar or energy during periods of low blood sugar causing symptoms like irritability and moodiness."

You are human. You ARE going to get hungry. So don't allow a failure to plan healthy snacks curdle encounters with colleagues and friends. Stick to the rules of the jungle: keep calm, share your bananas, and refrain from patronizing Krispy Kreme shops. And, do your part for world peace: load up a small cooler with the foods that boost serotonin intake such as pumpkin seeds, walnuts, almonds, avocado, dates, bananas, rolled oats, peanut butter, almond butter, fruits and veggies, whole grain crackers, deli turkey, cottage cheese, and chocolate milk (and a bit of dark chocolate won't hurt either), and keep it at the ready.

JINGLE JANGLE

DECEMBER 13, 2012

For better or worse, the holiday season can really throw the schedule off—the lists are long and the time is short. Now is a good moment to reflect upon what brings us real joy and let the rest go. A goal for making our homes feel like a cozy haven is that we have time to sink into the comfort we have created and experience a buffer against the holiday jingle and jangle.

Delicious meals are essential to this process. It's cold outside; we need to eat well to maintain stamina and good humor, so plan meals with care. Personally, I think there is nothing finer than a simple roasted chicken (paired with a fruity shiraz) for dinner. It perfumes the air with citrus, herb, and garlic, it is cheap, and it feeds many (even fussy guests.) Supplement it with easy, creamy pasta and you are more than halfway to bliss. So, don't get your tinsel in a tangle this holiday season. When you make time to relish the joy all will be merry and bright, even if every little detail is not just right.

SIMPLE ROASTED HERB CHICKEN

Choose a plump bird, note cooking directions & weight, unwrap, discard giblets, and rinse under cool water. Place in a roasting pan and sprinkle salt all over the skin. Stuff the bird with a big lemon or orange that has been sliced in half, a few garlic cloves, and a handful of rosemary, sage and/or thyme. This step can be prepared 2 days ahead. Roast the chicken (20 min/lb) in a 375°F oven.

CREAMY GOAT CHEESE PASTA

This simple sauce is amazingly versatile. Prepared a day ahead (or even frozen) it is best on whole-wheat penne pasta (16–24 ounces) boiled for 12 minutes.

In a food processor or blender mince 3–garlic cloves and the peel of one lemon. Add 2–cups fresh basil leaves; 8–ounces creamy goat cheese, ½–cup milk, and the juice from the lemon. Blend 30 seconds until a thick sauce forms; season with sea salt and fresh pepper. Toss sauce with hot pasta. Recipes serve 6.

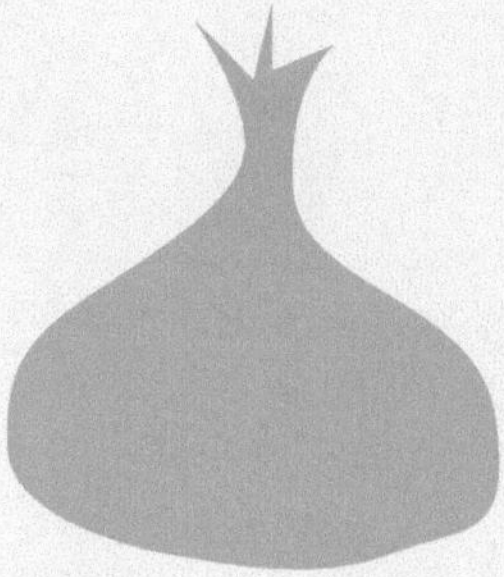

2013

PANTRY PRIORITIES

JANUARY 13, 2013

During deep winter few things make me happier than making tomato soup and setting in a supply of olive oil and chocolate. It gives me a feeling of security, like that stack of firewood out on our snow-frosted deck.

When stocking up the pantry, it is easy to take for granted all of the possibilities that a local supermarket affords. At the same time, I know that many folks lack the security of a full pantry and struggle on a modest winter grocery budget. The Williston Community Food Shelf does an outstanding job bridging the gap for our hungry neighbors, yet the need for assistance is growing everyday. According to WFS Volunteer Sally Stockwell Metro "Each month for the past six months we have had increasing numbers of family visits. We now see around 240 family visits a month (our families can come twice a month, and about 75 of them do come twice), representing over 800 individuals."

Now that the holidays have passed, it's a good time to take stock of our pantries and priorities, and to help others do so as well. Checks, gift cards to local supermarkets, and pasta sauce, cereal, peanut butter, jelly, canned fruits, veggies, and soup are the most helpful items to contribute. Visit willistonfoodshelf.com for hours of operation and volunteer opportunities. Assisting the hungry is a form of sacred activism—please consider a donation to your local food shelf today.

HEARTY TOMATO SOUP

This soup is heavenly paired with toasted English muffins topped with melted cheese.

Heat 2–T of vegetable oil in a soup pot. Dice two large onions and sauté, stirring often with a wooden spoon, 15–20 minutes, until caramelized. Deglaze the pot with 1–cup of chicken stock. Add 5–minced garlic cloves; two 28–ounce cans of crushed tomato; 1–cup orange juice; 4–cups of chicken stock; and ⅓-c vodka, Let the soup simmer 10 minutes. Taste and adjust for seasoning with salt and pepper. Add 1–cup of chopped fresh basil. (If you prefer a creamy soup, add 1–cup cream after heat is off.) Serves 10.

SPARKS OF INSPIRATION

JANUARY 31, 2013

Deep winter. Every afternoon around five, when the sun sinks below the horizon and the room suddenly feels chilly, I start to fantasize about the evening ahead: a roaring fire and a delicious meal to cap the day. The cold weather doesn't seem so dreary when I know there is something bubbling in the oven.

For inspiration I often turn to Eating Well's *Comfort Foods Made Healthy* by Jessie Price. It's a wonderful source for nostalgic eating that maintains the figure even during Vermont's long hibernation. The Turkey-Stuffed Portabella Mushrooms are especially fabulous; I would serve these for any occasion. Quick to prepare, they burst out of the oven ooeey-gooey mouth-wateringly gorgeous, ready to fill the stomach up, not out.

Served with a simple arugula salad these Turkey Burgers will more than satisfy. Add some roasted sweet potatoes, and you are well on the way to creating a new family favorite. The best part? You can season and stud the burgers with just about any combination of your favorite ingredients. That's pretty darn good inspiration—for deep winter.

TURKEY STUFFED PORTABELLA MUSHROOMS

(Adapted from *Comfort Foods Made Healthy*)

Heat oven to 400°F. Slice a large sweet onion lengthwise and sauté in 1–T of olive oil for about 20 minutes, until caramelized. Deglaze with 2–t cider vinegar. Reserve.

Meanwhile, in a mini-chopper mince together 3–garlic cloves along with the zest of 1–orange and some rosemary leaves. Place 1–pound of lean ground turkey in a prep bowl. Knead in rosemary mixture along with two large pinches of salt and a pinch of red pepper flakes. Form six burgers.

You'll need 6–Portabella mushroom caps, de-stemmed and wiped clean with a paper towel. Rub mushroom caps on both sides with Worcestershire sauce. Place one turkey ball in the center of each cap and gently press to fill the cap. Place on a baking sheet.

Bake on bottom rack about 20 minutes. Remove from the oven and top the burgers with the onion mixture. Top with some shredded fontina cheese. Bake 10 minutes more until cheese is bubbling. Serves 6.

CARIBBEAN CELEBRITY CHEFS

FEBRUARY 23, 2013

Around this time of year I default to happiness. Good-bye resolutions, Hello fine food! This year I was lucky to do it in style traveling to the Caymen Cookout with Vermont Creamery rock star Bob Reese, and family. It's the closest I'll ever get to being 'with the band', but I'll take it.

From the get-go, flutes of Tattinger flowed and our job was to chat up celebrity chefs Eric Ripert (Le Bernadin), Jose Andres (MiniBar) and Anthony Bourdain (well, you know). Top Chef Spike Mendelshon whipped up Asian duck and lamb loin-shank while Eleven Madison Park marvel, Daniel Humm, did a demo with strawberry gazpacho. There was a brigade of James Beard Winners, each trying to out-cook the other at events held morning, noon, and night. This was the Superbowl of Foodies—did I have the chops to survive six days of debauchery? (caymencookout.com)

I have so much respect for food professionals. I doubt you will find a more devoted, passionate, skilled group of fun people in any industry. These folks work hard, and their work is their play. The proof really is in their pudding.

What did I learn at this glorified frat party? Pureed Cauliflower and Grits are the new mashed potato. Tuna and foie gras taste really great together. Burgers can be Crab, Shrimp & Scallop, or Black Bean—the key is to douse them in a savory-sweet sauce on fresh brioche buns.

Combine quinoa and tabouli for an unforgettable crunchy grain salad. When it comes to fish, fresh is best—lemon, butter, and salt, that's it. And don't be stingy with oil, salt, or butter, chefs are generous with the stuff and that's why their food tastes so good! What I learned is when something tastes delicious, a few bites are all you need. The palate and the body are instantly alerted to goodness and become satisfied quickly. That's the real secret of great cooking.

PUREED CAULIFLOWER

De-stem the base and chop up two heads of white cauliflower. Place veg in a soup pot, along with 8–garlic cloves; and 32–ounces of chicken stock. Cover and simmer until the cauliflower is soft enough to blend with immersion blender. Add 4–T butter and puree until silky. Season for taste.

WHAT'S IN A NAME?

MARCH 14, 2013

Many cultures have wonderful names for things that we simply don't enjoy in English. For example, my favorite Arabic word is "taraadin" which implies a happy solution for everyone: I win, you win. The Spanish have the delightful "duende" which blends the thrill of passion, energy, and artistic excellence together. The German "korinthenkacker" literally means raisin-pooper; it's their humorous moniker for a pencil-pushing control freak. While English shares the word "aware", the Japanese use it to convey an appreciation of the ephemeral beauty of the world. "Aware" is that poignant sensation that time is passing and the cycle of life is inevitable, especially as the season changes.

I also love the Japanese word "Okonomiyaki" (Oh-ko-no-mi-yaki). Say that three times fast! These are crêpe-style pancakes, studded with shrimp or chicken, and ribbons of scallion and cabbage. They are fun to say, fun to make, and fun to eat. The name is derived from "okonomi" meaning "as you like it" and "yaki" which means grilled or cooked. Sometimes called Japanese pizza, the pancakes are soothing and hearty—the perfect springtime comfort food. My version is not necessarily authentic, possible combinations are as varied as what's leftover in your fridge. Simply make it as you like it.

SPICY SAUCE

Whisk together ½–cup mayonnaise; 2–T soy sauce; and 2–t sriracha sauce (or to taste). Reserve. Pan toast 2–T sesame seeds until golden brown. Reserve separately.

OKONOMIYAKI (JAPANESE PANCAKES)

Whisk together 5–eggs; 1–t soy sauce; 1–t sesame oil, 1–t sea salt; and ⅓–cup flour. Stir in 2–cups thinly chopped cabbage; 4–scallions, trimmed and sliced; ¾–cup cooked, chopped shrimp.

In a large non-stick skillet, on medium-hi heat, warm 2–t coconut oil until it glistens. Ladle the batter in batches just like you would for small pancakes. Cook each side 3 minutes until golden brown. Repeat the process, adding more oil if needed.

Reserve the cooked pancakes on an ovenproof platter, covered in a 200ºF oven, until all the pancakes are cooked. Scatter sesame seeds over the platter of Okonomiyaki, and serve with the spicy sauce. Yield: 12 pancakes.

TRANSI-TIONS

APRIL 18, 2013

As we jump full force into spring cleanup projects, it's wise to remember that there will be a rogue day or two when it is still bone-cracking cold outside. Despite our bodies' attempt to transition to lighter foods, these are the days that we still crave warmth and sustenance. Be prepared for this culinary contradiction, and I promise that you will be richly rewarded.

I like to keep something at the ready that involves melted gooey cheese; that usually does the trick for me. Think grilled Panini or a quick flatbread pizza with a side bowl of steaming soup. The good news is that it's possible to enjoy these hearty foods with a lighter, healthier twist.

BACON & BLEU CHEESE FLATBREAD

By choosing flavorful turkey bacon and a small amount of pungent cheese, you'll enjoy lean protein and satisfying flavor with minimal calories. Choose store-bought whole wheat; knead a 1–teaspoon of cornmeal into the dough as you prep it. Roll it out on a cookie sheet lined with parchment. Top the dough with 5–strips of turkey bacon, sprinkle 4–ounces of crumbled bleu cheese. (Prep this before you set out to do chores for a few hours).

About 20 minutes before the hunger-pains hit, heat oven to 425°F. Bake the flatbread for 12 minutes. While the flatbread cooks, toss a generous handful of fresh arugula with 1–T of olive oil. When the flatbread is ready, top the surface with the greens, cut into six portions; serve immediately.

TURKEY CHEDDAR AVOCADO PANINI

A good grilled sandwich, like Turkey Cheddar Avocado Panini, requires decent equipment. I love my Cusinart 'griddler gourmet' because there is no prepping of the bread with extra calories, like butter or oil. In just minutes it toasts the outside to a perfect golden crunch as it melts the gooey cheese.

Choose a square-shaped whole-wheat roll designed for panini. Slice open the roll and add a thick slice of turkey breast, a slice of cheddar, and a little ripe avocado. Prep the panini early, set in fridge covered in plastic, and 20 minutes before break–time heat up the griddler. You'll be transitioned to nirvana before you know it.

HUMBLE CRUMBLE PIE

MAY 30, 2013

For happy people, the word "problem" is rarely part of the vocabulary. A problem is viewed as a drawback, a struggle, or an unstable situation while a challenge is viewed as something positive like an opportunity, a task, or a dare. In other words, it's not what happens, it is how we interpret what happens. How does this relate to cooking? Read on.

I decided to treat my pals to a simple fruit crostata. I have made this crust a hundred times, a no brainer. But, when I rolled out the dough, something was funky—too hard and dry. Pressed for time, I turned to plan 'B' and coaxed the naughty stuff into a baking dish. I filled it with fresh cherries, rhubarb, and strawberries and baked it open-faced. When I pulled it from the oven, the pie was U-G-L-Y! Humbled, I moved on to plan 'C' (for Crumble). Butter, sugar, flour, oats, and another 15 minutes bake time did the trick, and the maple-glazed walnuts, didn't hurt, either.

It takes guts and good ingredients to turn a disaster into something tasty, so whenever you face a cooking obstacle, try seeing it as a challenge. I was humbled until some simple crumble (and really good maple ice cream) saved my day.

HUMBLE CRUMBLE PIE

When moderation won't do, this is the dessert for you

Preheat oven to 375°F. Pulse together 3½–cups white pastry flour and 1–stick Crisco. Add a pinch of salt and just enough water to form the dough. Wrap in plastic and chill. Coat 2–cups of walnuts with ½–cup maple syrup; bake on a covered cookie sheet for 15 minutes. Remove and sprinkle nuts with a bit of sea salt.

Pit 2–cups fresh cherries; dice 3–cups fresh rhubarb and strawberries each. Combine fruit in a prep bowl; toss with 2–egg yolks, and ½–cup cornstarch and sugar each.

Press dough into a 14x9x2" baking dish (up the sides.) Add fruit and bake 45 minutes.

In a mini-processor, pulse 4–ounces of cold butter with ½–cup sugar and flour each; combine this with 2–cups oats to make the crumble. Top pie with crumble and some walnuts; bake 15–20 minutes.

RAIN PAIN

JULY 11, 2013

Burlington's summer of 2013 is the wettest consecutive stretch of weather on record, with about 20" of rain. If summer ever actually arrives it sure would be fun to serve something to celebrate the berry crop. A creamy, crunchy fruit tart will be at the top of my list when the sun decides to shine. This recipe is layered with sunny lemon curd and creamy mascarpone and the results are simply delightful.

ALMOND BERRY TART

Tart Crust: in a food processor pulse the zest of one lemon until finely minced. Add 1–cup almonds; ½–cup sugar; and a pinch of salt; and pulse until a fine meal forms. Add 1–c flour (gluten-free works, too); 1–t almond extract; 4–ounces cold cubed butter; and ¼–cup water. Pulse together until a sticky dough forms. Wrap dough in plastic and freeze for 30 minutes. Preheat oven to 375°F. Working quickly, press the dough into an 8" or 9" tart pan with a removable bottom pressing dough up the sides. Bake for 20 minutes, cool in the pan.

LEMON CURD & CREAMY MASCARPONE

While the crust bakes, prepare the lemon curd (can do ahead 1–day). In a saucepan combine 3–egg yolks; zest of a lemon; ¼–cup of lemon juice; and 6–T of sugar in a small saucepan. Whisk to combine. Over medium heat, stir it constantly with a wooden spoon. Cook until mixture is thick enough to coat back of the wooden spoon, 5–7 minutes. Remove saucepan from heat. Add 4–ounces of chilled butter, one large cube at a time, stirring until the consistency is smooth. Transfer curd to a medium bowl. Lay a sheet of plastic wrap directly onto the surface of the curd to avoid a skin from forming. Chill at least 1 hour.

For the creamy filling whip 8–ounces of whipping cream together with 1–t vanilla and 2–T confectionary sugar until fluffy. Then, quickly beat in 8–ounces of mascarpone cheese. Chill until ready to complete tart.

When the crust is cooled, gently remove it from the pan and place on a round platter. Fill the tart with lemon curd and then layer on the creamy mascarpone. Top with fresh seasonal berries. Serves 12.

WE NEED TO TALK ABOUT ZUCCHINI

AUGUST 13, 2013

Zucchini is equal parts ubiquitous and astonishing in its volume and versatility. The question is not how to use zucchini, but how many ways can it be used to showcase its muscular goodness. Sliced raw and doused simply with olive oil and shaved Asiago, it is the kind of dish that makes me swoon summer.

Ditto a cold mint-infused soup pulsing green and goodness. Zucchini morphs into another kind of heaven altogether fried in tempura batter, with sprinkles of truffle salt and a side of garlicky aioli. Swimming in baked Parmesan discs, it's a stupefying snack that may require an intervention.

I made a huge batch of these the other day, then headed out to girl's night. When I returned, I asked my husband how he liked the new treat. He said, "They were really good, but a little rich." A glance at the empty platter–there had been enough servings for six people–told me all I needed to know about my favorite new recipe.

ZUCCHINI PARMESAN DISCS

Preheat over to 375°F. Combine 1–cup hand-shredded Parmesan with 2–T shredded zucchini. Cover a cookie sheet with parchment paper. Place quarter-sized mounds of the mixture onto the sheet, spacing 3" apart. Bake 8–10 minutes until edges are golden. Cool and eat like mini-pizzas.

FRIED ZUCCHINI

I tried these two ways, in a heavy cast-iron pan, with pleasantly different results. Canola oil on the stove: lower smoke point, zucchini tastes like French fries. Grapeseed oil on the grill: higher smoke point, cooks a little slower, zucchini tastes like tempura.

Layer a cookie sheet with paper towel. Heat oven to 200°F. In a medium bowl, whisk together 1 ¼–cup flour and white wine each. In another medium bowl mix ½–cup flour with large pinches of salt and pepper. Slice zucchini into 3" lengths, medium thickness (one medium feeds two.) Heat 2–cups of oil; when it sizzles, toss 4–6 pieces into the seasoned flour, then into the batter. Fry, turning once, until golden. Keep adding batches. Sprinkle with truffle or sea salt, keep warm in oven.

IT'S A TURKEY

NOVEMBER 14, 2013

Cooking a moist turkey takes time, but not much effort. Over the past several years the media, desperate to spin holiday frenzy, has gobbledygook the simple task of cooking a bird into a national obsession. Brining, basting, frying, stuffing? What's a host to do? For starters, relax—it's *a turkey!*

Here's a simple guide to get your bird going; in the meantime, quaff a few glasses, kick back, and enjoy the holiday.

Two hours before cook time make sure you have a defrosted bird (12–14 pounds), a heavy-duty roasting pan lined with a roasting rack, and an oven big enough to hold it. Collaborate with a family member to manage the day's schedule and cooking time, about 2 ½ to 3 hours. Place the turkey in the pan, remove and reserve the giblet packet, and wipe the bird down with paper towel.

Because there is air circulation within the cavity, unstuffed turkey cooks more evenly, and faster, than a stuffed turkey; stuffing the bird also poses significant food-safety challenges. Instead, stuff 4–orange halves into the cavity along with a fistful of herbs (rosemary, sage, thyme) and some peeled garlic. Sprinkle all over with kosher salt. Use soap and hot water to wash down everything the bird has come in contact with. Preheat the oven to 450°F for at least 30 minutes.

When it's time to roast, place the turkey in the oven, add 2–cups of chicken or turkey stock to the pan, and reduce the oven to 350°F. Cook the bird; no looking, no basting.

When your timekeeper says it's OK (and various parts of the bird all register 165°F on a meat thermometer) remove the pan from the oven. Carefully lift the turkey and roasting rack onto a large platter. Reserve the pan drippings for the gravy. Tent the turkey in heavy-duty foil. Allow the turkey to rest, up to an hour. In the meantime, the stuffing and other side dishes can heat up in the oven while you make the gravy.

For more detailed roasting tips and exceptional gravy, consult Williston's award-winning cookbook author Molly Stevens,' *All About Roasting*. Happy Thanksgiving to everyone!

2014

RESTOR-ATIVE POWER

JANUARY 14, 2014

To me there are few things better than a hearty bowl of homemade soup. Such soup steams comfort and reassurance after the day's tribulations, and it provides consolation and companionship like no other food. In deep winter, this is exactly the Rx for cabin fever, achy joints, or a broken heart.

After clearing out mystery blocks of food in my freezer (leftovers from the holidays) I found some pretty good stuff to work with. Roasted butternut squash, cooked turkey meat, chicken stock and puree of parsnip. Hum. I started my soup dance and surprised my family with a comfort soup that easily doubles as the base for a healthy turkey potpie.

Try to use homemade chicken stock if at all possible—it is rich in magnesium, calcium, and many trace minerals that are easy for the body to absorb. The gelatin promotes healthy cartilage and supports the connective tissue that fights joint disease.

I served the soup with toasted honey-oat gluten-free bread from Barre's Vermont Gluten Free Bakery. It is so delicious that regular bread-eaters will enjoy it, too; it has a biscuit-like quality that beautifully complements the creamy soup.

TURKEY POT SOUP

Heat 1–T of olive oil in a large soup pot. Add 1–large chopped onion and sauté on medium heat for 20 minutes, stirring occasionally. Deglaze with ½–cup of sherry and scrape up the brown bits on the pot's bottom with a wooden spoon. Add 6–cups of homemade chicken stock; 2–cups chopped carrots; and 2–cups chopped celery. Simmer 10 minutes.

Fill another pan with 5–chopped potatoes (skin on), barely cover with water, and simmer for 25 minutes. Add 4–T butter and salt & pepper to taste. Gently smash the potatoes with a potato masher until slightly lumpy. Add the potatoes and liquids to the soup pot.

Rough chop 4–cups cooked turkey or chicken meat. Add to soup pot. (I added 1–cup butternut squash and 1–cup of parsnip puree here, but this step is optional.) Simmer the batch for 10 minutes. Add 2–cups frozen peas. Adjust for seasoning with salt and pepper. Serves 12.

GO WITH YOUR GUT

MARCH 13, 2014

'Healthy' and 'good health' are cherished words, but what do they really mean? I had the opportunity to attend Kripalu's Healthy Living Detox Retreat with Dr. John Bagnulo in Pittsfield, MA, recently. Dr. Bagnulo was expert at translating nutrition science from the lab to the kitchen, and I peppered him with cook's questions.

We learned that our gut is where the action is. Because our digestive system is the boss of bodily functions and disease prevention, it is the key to optimal health. Our belly demands respect from the food we eat, or nasty consequences occur—heartburn, flatulence, and much worse. Did you know that most chronic and acute diseases are complicated by poor gut health?

"On a spectrum gluten-sensitivity affects everyone; this is not a fad, but an evolving reality. Due to food processing and GMO's (genetically modified organisms) what used to be 23% gluten in our food is now 66%, and our digestive system simply cannot handle the daily overload. Rid toxic grains such as wheat, rye, barley, oats, spelt, and kamut from your diet" advises Dr. Bagnulo.

Instead, choose easily digested, organic and local foods that are nutrient dense. Your plate should be 25% protein, 55% vegetable, and 20% fruit. Full fats like grass-fed butter, and olive and coconut oils are vital for better brain function. Super foods like wild-caught fish, leafy greens, free-range eggs, blueberries, seaweed, cacao, and garlic are good choices. If you choose grains, amaranth, buckwheat, quinoa, millet are okay—in moderation—along with pinto and cannellini beans, sprouted lentils and brown rice. Eating gluten-free products is healthier only if the delivery is nutrient-dense: think poached eggs on buttered GF toast, *not* GF cupcakes.

The best book I have found that summarizes Dr. Bagnulo's message is *Practical Paleo* by Diane Sanfilippo, BS, NC. The book is less about cave man eating than it is about cultivating healthy habits. It has scientific explanations and practical suggestions for gut health, organ function, and product choices as it relates to actual eating. The book is filled with excellent charts, colorful illustrations, and recipes that make learning about optimal health a gut.

DAILY ORGANIC CREAMY GREEN SMOOTHIE

You will eat many more F&V than if you chewed these, so that is the benefit of a smoothie breakfast; keep smoothies to one meal a day so that enzymes can do their job in the chewing process.

In a Vitamix, combine the following organic foods: ½-avocado (glutathione); ½-unpeeled lemon, 1–cup frozen strawberries (potassium, elegiac acid), 1–chunk cucumber (citrulline), 1–fist of spinach & kale each (glutathione, potassium, alkaline), 2–stalks celery (nitrates), 2–ounces ginger. Water if needed. Drink 16–ounces every morning.

HOW TO COOK A KID

ESSAY FROM 2005

The important things I've needed to know I first learned in a kitchen. I've learned that recipes are guidelines for creativity, not rigid rules. I've learned to provision myself with quality ingredients and tools, and that a bit of knowledge empowers a cook exponentially. I know that foods have a natural affinity for each other and it is nature's way to align strengths. I know that less is often more.

I have learned about love in the kitchen, too—this is where I vetted my man. The magic of a romance could easily blossom or fade during dinner prep as I carefully weighed and measured the sexual chemistry in the kitchen, a reliable harbinger of how things might go in the bedroom. As friendly acquaintances we'd connect through a desire to spend time and the shared passion for a good meal, which, in turn, might spread to the heart, and, if the cooking was delicious, perhaps even become a string of pleasant memories. I would surreptitiously watch my candidate—was he careful not to bruise the garlic? Did he treat the wine with proper reverence, as the living thing it was? What did his profile look like as a spoonful of sauce pooled upon his lips?

These considerations rewarded me, and the man with the most genuine vigor, the purest of motives, the heartiest of appetites eventually won a permanent seat at my table; he's been showing up for dinner now for more than two decades. He is not my soul mate, for it is not enough to say that he inhabits only a part of me. He is my gentle silhouette, offering honest reflection and the freedom of friendly boarders. We have lived together in equal amounts of satisfaction and lust longer than our original families held us close. And everyday, when we sit down to share a meal, I am replenished with the knowledge that he knows me and celebrates me like no one else on the planet.

That we humans love deeply, often irrevocably, is understood, and the rituals we choose to define our families is how that love is seasoned. Since college I have been meditating, and when our firstborn was an infant I was pleased to continue my practice, taking thirty precious minutes every afternoon to go deep: to rest my mind, to reconnect my body to my soul. While our home was a child-centered one, we were careful to avoid a child-dominated one. My mothering mantra was "there is life after birth" and that meant me, too, so I established structures to honor us all. For me, it was my daily retreat, which in turn, became a gift to my children. My baby, safely gated within her room and free to explore, would rest or do whatever fed her until it was time for her rosebud lips to reconnect with my bounty. When her sisters came along the pattern continued, part of each afternoon devoted to a period of quiet time, each individual charged with finding her own peace.

Afterward we would gather in the kitchen for food, chosen at my discretion, but offered in a smorgasbord of choices from the earliest moments. The sisters had authority over their needs and desires, even if it meant that one child ate carrots for a solid week and only chicken the next—that was what her growing body called out for and I trusted Mother Nature to round things out by month's end. Food was always a playground for us, never a battlefield; I taught them that their body is a wonderland, not an amusement park.

I had a few kitchen rules for myself that worked nicely, too. First and foremost, I resisted the urge to do anything for my children that they could manage on their own. Next, I tried to say yes as often as possible; I let them touch everything—but with only one (gentle) finger. I showed them respect and made respectful choices. And I took the time to train, teaching them well, letting them lead the way. Finally, there was the when/then rule. As in "*when* the flour and the butter form little balls, *then* you can stir in the water; *when* the dishwasher is emptied *then* I can drive you to soccer practice." Easy as piecrust.

Human beings begin connected by an umbilical cord and then by heart-strings and finally by brain waves. The parenting process can be as slow and exhausting as a march through molasses. And just when we think we have no more reserves left, an amazing young person shows up bearing a bucket of hot water and a towel. Like ripening fruit almost ready to fall from a tree, our daughters are now fueling for independence—but their need for sustenance is more intense and complex than a mere meal can provide. The hunger is emotional and intellectual, economical and physical. They carelessly toss my heart through a meat grinder as easily as they peck me tenderly on the cheek. Their mouths receive, but they also provide: ripe and spicy opinions, requests and questions, all seasoned by the confidence of a connected soul. And sometimes they test the boundaries with bolder demands from bigger mouths that have burst past the protective fencing of braces and now graze comfortably among the kissing fields of their youth.

Sometimes I am asked "aren't you sad they are growing up so fast?" And I can truly say "No." It's not that I am unsentimental, rather, proud and grateful—for it is work well done, though never complete. We savor our licks of optimism and get on with our lives as the sisters make their way through the kitchen with equal doses of competence and compassion, cooking up something yummy with their young men along for the meal.

And through it all I meditate, and reflect on the contents and contentment in my heart. My dogs are my meditation partners now, their devotion fueled by their evening meal that follows our sessions. My husband and I again dine à deux, a twenty-plus-year kid-blitz that has spiraled us full circle, back to our courtship days in the kitchen.

When the daughters are about we manage to bite the tongues in our mouths, and reflect on wisdom gained: children cry wolf for simple reasons—out of fear, to test our limits, to gain a sense of reassurance. A misbehaving child is a discouraged child. Structure and ritual matter to them, it is something we all hunger for. Quality and consistency always count.

Like a good meal, loving takes planning, patience and practiced skills. The delicious result is a child who will always know how to handle herself—for she has learned the importance of feeding her mouth, her mind, and her soul.

RECIPE INDEX

2003

2004

2005

2006

2007

2008

2009

2010

2011

2012

2013

2014

CPSIA information can be obtained at www.ICGtesting.com
Printed in the USA
LVOW02s0914211114
414681LV00001B/1/P